PORTUGUESE
Phrase Book

ACKNOWLEDGEMENTS

I would like to thank everyone who had a hand in this book, especially Suami Tiago Mendes, who did much of the initial work on the layout, and Lizi Attwood, who tried out the strange language which appears in the third column and wrote a first approach to the data base.

This small work is dedicated to Judith and Chris, the best sisters anyone could wish for.

JOHN PELHAM

PORTUGUESE
Phrase Book

CLÁSSICA
EDITORA

Título: **Portuguese Phrase Book**

Autor: John Pelham

Copyright © by Clássica Editora, 2002, 2006
CE - Editores Associados, Lda
Rua do Vale Formoso, 37
1959-006 LISBOA
Tel 21 868 01 92 Fax 21 868 02 59
E-mail: classica@classica-editora.com

Capa:
Tiago Oliveira *(Designer Gráfico da Editora)*

Execução Gráfica:
JMM-Artes Gráficas, Lda.

Impressão e acabamento:
Manuel Barbosa & Filhos, Lda.

ISBN 989-604-012-5
ISBN-13: 978-989-604-012-3

Depósito Legal n.º 244 365/06

2.ª edição

Distribuição
DINTERNAL, Lda.

LISBOA:	Rua do Vale Formoso, 37	1959-006 LISBOA
	Telef.: +351 218 681 183	Fax + 351 218 681 257
	E-mail: dinternal@dinternal.pt	Portugal
PORTO:	Rua José Falcão, 188-1º	4050-315 PORTO
	Telef.: +351 223 322 232	Fax +351 222 008 050
	E-mail: britanica.por@dinternal.pt	Portugal

INDEX

1 - PRONUNCIATION

In the following chart, the combinations of letters used in the columns headed *Notation* are the closest to the sounds in Portuguese. In many cases a more accurate sound can only be made, especially for the nasals, by listening carefully to Portuguese people.

Letters in bold indicate where the stress falls. Unstressed vowels are sometimes practically lost: *pequeno* (small) becomes *p'kenoo, comida* (meal) becomes *k'meedah*.

The "h" in the *Notation* is not an aspirate, as in "**h**ot". It is used after the letter "a" to indicate that the sound is not the short "a" as in "fat" but a longer sound, closer to "far". The "h" is also used for the stressed "e" as in "café" (*kahfeh*).

Accents change the sound of a vowel or the stress of a word. In the interests of simplification, the sound changes have not been included, with the exception of the *é* (see the vowel sounds below). The stress change has been indicated by the bold print. For instance, in the list you will find *fluido (flooeedoo)* and *concluído (konklooeedoo)*.

Accents can also show a difference between words spelt the same (*da* - "of the", *dá* "give").

The closest sound in English	*Notation (sound)*	*Example (words)*	*Notation (words)*
Single vowels			
a like the **a** in "f**a**r" but shorter	*ah*	mala	*mahlah*
e[1] like the e in "f**e**d"	*e*	mel	*mel*
e mute at the end of a word	*'e*	creme	*crem'e*
é between "f**e**d" and "l**ay**"	*eh*	pé	*peh*
i between "sh**i**p" and "sh**ee**p"	*ee*	vir	*veer*
o like the **o** in "n**o**t"	*o*	nota	*notah*
o at the end of a word, as in "t**oo**"	*oo*	do	*doo*
u[2] like the **oo** in "t**oo**"	*oo*	azul	*azool*

---

[1] The word for **and** (the letter **e** by itself) is pronounced like the **i** in the list above.

[2] See also **gu-** and **qu-** in the consonant section.

The closest sound in English	*Notation (sound)*	*Example (words)*	*Notation (words)*
Two vowels together			
ae a combination of **a** and **e**	*ahe*	aeroporto	*aheroportoo*
ai like the **y** in "type"	*ahy*	pai	*pahy*
aí a combination of **a** and **ee**	*ahee*	país	*paheesh*
ao a combination of **a** and **o**	*aho*	ao	*aho*
au like the **ou** in "loud"	*ahoo*	saudar	*sahoodahr*
aú a combination of **a** and **oo**	*ahoo*	saúde	*sahood'e*
ei like the **ay** in "lay"	*ay*	leite	*layt'e*
eu a sound like the **ey** and **ou** in "Hey you" glided together.	*eyoo*	meu	*meyoo*
ia like the **ea** in "fear"	*eeah*	tia	*teeah*
ie a combination of the **ee** in "sheep" and the **c** in "fed"	*ee-e*	dieta	*dee-etah*
io a combination of the **ee** in "sheep" and the **oo** in "too"	*eeoo*	tio	*teeoo*

	The closest sound in English	*Notation (sound)*	*Example (words)*	*Notation (words)*
iu	as above but with the stress on the **oo**	*eeoo*	viu	*veeoo*
oi	when one syllable, like the **oy** in "b**oy**"	*oy*	boi	*boy*
oi	when more than one syllable, this is a combination of **o** and **ee**	*oee*	proibido	*proeebeedoo*
oo	this is two sounds, the short and long **o**	*o-oo*	enjoo	*enjo-oo*
ou	like the **oo** in "d**oo**r", but shorter	*oh*	outono	*ohtonoo*
ua	a combination of the **oo** in "f**oo**d" and the **a** in "f**a**r"	*ooah*	lua	*looah*
ue	a combination of the **oo** in "f**oo**d" and the **e** in "f**e**d"	*ooe*	cruel	*krooel*
ui	a combination of the **oo** in "f**oo**d" and the **ee** in "sh**ee**p"	*ooee*	fluido	*flooeedoo*
uí	as above but with the stress on **ee**	oo*ee*	concluído	*conclooeedoo*

10

The closest sound in English	*Notation (sound)*	*Example (words)*	*Notation (words)*

Nasal vowels[3]

ã	like the **an** in "s**ang**" but nasalised	*ah~*	amanhã	*ahmanya~*
ãe,	like the **a** in "**a**ncient" - nasalised	*ayn~*	mãe	*mayn~*
em	like the **ai** in "g**ai**n" - nasalised		além	*alayn~*
ão,	like the **ow** in "t**ow**n" - nasalised	*aw~*	acção	*ahssaw~*
am			partiram	*pahrteeraw~*
im	like the **in** in "b**in**go" - nasalised	*een~*	fim	*feen~*
õe	like the **oi** in "c**oi**n" - nasalised	*oyn~*	põe	*poyn~*
om	like the **on** in "l**on**g" - nasalised	*on~*	bom	*bon~*
um	like the **oo** in "s**oo**n" - nasalised	*oon~*	atum	*atoon~*

---

[3] The *til* (~) symbolises the nasal sound

The closest sound in English	*Notation (sound)*	*Example (words)*	*Notation (words)*
Consonants[4]			
c 1 - hard before **-a, -o, -u**, as in "**c**at"	*k*	vaca	*vahkah*
2 - soft before **-e** and **-i**, as in "**s**it"	*ss*	alface	*ahlfahss'e*
ch 1 - like the **sh** in "**sh**e"	*sh*	cheque	*shek'e*
ch 2 - (only in foreign words) like the **ch** in "**ch**in"	*ch*	ciao[5]	*chahoo*
ç like the **s** in sit	*ss*	almoçar	*ahlmossahr*
g 1 - hard before **-a, -o, -u**, as in "**g**ot"	*g*	golo	*golo*
2 - soft before **-e, -i**, as in "leisure"	*j*	agir	*ajeer*
gu 1 - as in "i**gu**ana"	*gw*	água	*ahgwah*
gu 2 - hard before **e**, with the **u** mute	*gu*	sangue	*ssangu'e*
h mute	—	hora	*orah*

---

[4] Those not in the list are broadly the same as in English

[5] Sometimes spelt "tchau"

12

	The closest sound in English	*Notation (sound)*	*Example (words)*	*Notation (words)*
j	like the **s** in "leisure"	*j*	hoje	*oj'e*
lh	similar to the **lli** "million" - much shorter than in "billy"	*ly*	bilhete	*beelyet'e*
nh	similar to the **ney** in "vineyard"	*ny*	vinho	*veenyoo*
p	mute before **t**	—	óptimo	*oteemoo*
qu	1 - before -**a,** -**o** the sound is like **qu** in "**qu**estion"	*kw*	quando	*kwahndoo*
	2 - hard before -**e** and -**i**, as in "**c**at"	*k*	pequeno[6]	*pekenoo*
r	1 - at the start of a word or written **rr**, it is pronounced as in French	*rr*	rato	*rrahtoo*
			horror	*orror*
	2 - in the middle or at the end of a word, there is a slight trill	*r*	arte	*ahrt'e*

---

[5]Note that this is <u>not</u> pronounced *pekwenoo*

	The closest sound in English	*Notation (sound)*	*Example (words)*	*Notation (words)*
s	1 - like the **s** in "sit" when it comes at the start of word or is written **ss**	*ss*	sal	*ssahl*
			assar	*ahssahr*
	2 - like the **zz** in "bu**zz**" when it is in the middle of a word	*z*	casa	*kahzah*
	3 - like the **sh** in "**ash**" at the end of	*sh*	casas	*kahzash*
	a word and before **m**, **p**, **t**, **v** or the **k**		desporto	*deshportoo*
	sound		hospital	*oshpeetahl*
x	1 - as -**ch** above (=*sh*)	*sh*	taxa	*tahshah*
	2 - like the x in "ma**x**imum"[7]	*ks*	fax	*fahks*
	3 - like the **zz** in "bu**zz**"	*z*	exame	*ezahm'e*
z	like the **zz** in bu**zz**	*z*	zero	*zeroo_*

---

[7] Only found in foreign words

2 - PHRASES AND NOTES FOR TRAVELLERS

GENERAL INTRODUCTION

You might like to look quickly at the "Learning and improving" part of this Phrase Book to get an overall idea of the language from the start. Note that the masculine / feminine concept is important for everything you say – for example, a simple expression of thanks ("Thank you", "Thank you very much") involves making the distinction between the genders (*Obrigado* for men, *Obrigada* for women).

1 - AT THE AIRPORT

There are air services to Lisbon, Oporto, Faro and the Atlantic islands (Madeira and the Azores) provided by most international airlines, both regular services and charter. Customs clearance is normally limited to spot checks and there is no limit to goods such as wine or tobacco to take back to other European Union countries, provided they are for personal use. The official currency is the euro.

Useful related topics in the vocabulary section: Air travel (1); numbers (11); personal details (12); telling the time (18).

Where's the information desk?	Onde é o balcão de informações?	*Onde eh oo bahlkaw~ de eenformahssoyn~sh?*
Is there a bank here / at the airport?	Há algum banco aqui / no aeroporto?	*Ah ahlgoon~ bahnkoo ahkee / noo aheroportoo?*
Have you got a ticket in the name of ...	Tem um bilhete em nome de…?	*Tayn~ oon~ beelyet'e ayn nom'e de …?*
I'd like a window seat, please.	Queria um lugar à janela, por favor.	*Kereeah oon~ loogahr a jahnelah, por fahvor.*
Where can I get a taxi?	Onde posso apanhar um táxi?	*Onde possoo ahpahnyahr oon~ tahksee?*
Is there a bus service into town?	Há um serviço de autocarros para a cidade?	*Ah oon~ sserveessoo de ahootokahrroos pahrah ah sseedahde?*

Where is the check-in?	Onde é o check-in?	*Onde eh oo shek-een?*
Which gate is the flight to ...?	Qual é a porta do voo para ...?	*Kwahl eh ah portah do vo-oo pahrah ...?*
When does the plane leave?	Quando é que o avião parte?	*Kwahndoo eh ke oo ahveeaw~ pahrt'e?*
When does the plane from ... arrive?	Quando chega o avião vindo de ...?	*Kwahndoo shegah oo ahveeaw~ veendoo de ...?*

What you might hear

Ali. / Por ali.	Over there. / That way.
À direita.	On the right.
À esquerda.	On the left.
Lá fora.	Outside.
Já não há.	There're none left.

2

17

2 - SIMPLE CONVERSATION

The Portuguese are very formal when they address you. Anyone with a university degree is known as *Doutor* or *Doutora*. It is also common to hear *Senhor Engenheiro* when someone is addressing an engineer. You will find that people you get to know will use the third person (if you are not well one day and someone you have met sees you the next day, he or she will ask you *"Como está?"* or *"Como vai?"* not *"Como estás?"* or *"Como vais?"*). See the Learning and Improving section (point 9) for more detail.

Useful related topics in the vocabulary section: Days, months, seasons and special dates (6); time phrases (18); the weather (20).

Hello.	Olá	*Olah*
Good morning / afternoon / evening.	Bom dia / boa tarde / boa noite	*Bon~ deeah / boah tard' / Boa noyt'e*
How are you?	Como está?	*Komoo eshtah?*

2

What's your name?	Como é que se chama?	*Komoo eh ke se shahmah?*
My name's ...	Chamo-me…	*Shahmoo-me...*
Where are you from?	De onde é?	*De onde eh?*
I come from...	Eu sou de…	*Eyoo ssoh de...*
Please.	Por favor	*Por fahvor*
Thank you.	Obrigado / Obrigada	*Obreegahdoo / Obreegahduh*
Thank you very much.	Muito obrigado / obrigada	*Mooeentoo obreegahdoo / obreegahdah*
I don't understand.	Não percebo.	*Naw~ persseboo.*
Can you speak more slowly?	Pode falar mais devagar?	*Pod'e fahlahr mahysh devahgahr?*
Could you help me / show me the way to ...?	Pode ajudar-me? / indicar-me o caminho para…?	*Pod'e ahjoodahr-me? / eendeekahr-me oo kahmoonyoo pahrah ...?*
How much is ... / are ... ?	Quanto custa …? / custam …?	*Kwahntoo koostah ...? / koostaw~ ...?*

What is there to see here?	O que há para ver aqui?	*Oo ke ah pahrah ver ahkee?*
I don't speak any Portuguese.	Não falo português.	*Naw~ fahloo portooguesh.*
I know a few words.	Sei algumas palavras.	*Ssay ahlgoomahsh pahlahvrahsh.*
I have been in Portugal for 2 / 3 days.	Estou em Portugal há dois / três dias.	*Eshtoh ayn~ Portoogahl a doysh / tresh deeahsh.*
I have two brothers / two sisters.	Tenho dois irmãos / duas irmãs.	*Tenyoo dois eermaw~sh / dooahsh eermah~sh.*
I'm with my partner / husband.	Estou com o meu companheiro / marido.	*Eshtoh kon~ oo meyoo kompahnyayroo / mahreedoo.*
I'm with my partner / wife.	Estou com a minha companheira / mulher.	*Eshtoh kon~ ah meenyah kompanyayrah / moolyer*
Are you here on your own?	Está aqui sozinho / sozinha?	*Eshtah ahkee ssozeenyoo / ssozeenyah?*

2

English	Portuguese	Pronunciation
I'm single / married / divorced. (a man speaking)	Sou solteiro / casado / divorciado.	*Ssoh ssoltayroo / kahzahdoo / deevorsseeahdoo.*
(a woman speaking)	Sou solteira / casada / divorciada.	*Ssoh ssoltayrah /kahzada / deevorsseeahdah*
I'm ... years old.	Tenho … anos.	*Tenyoo … ahnoosh.*
How old are you?	Quantos anos tem?	*Kwahntoos ahnoos tayn~?*
I live in ...	Vivo em …	*Veevoo ayn~ ...*
I am a student.	Sou estudante.	*Ssoh eshtoodahnt'e.*
I work in ...	Trabalho em …	*Trahbahlyoo ayn~ ...*
I'm sorry, can you repeat that?	Desculpe, pode repetir?	*Deshkoolpe, pod'e repeteer?*
Goodbye.	Adeus.	*Ahdayoosh.*
See you later.	Até logo.	*Ahteh logoo.*
See you tomorrow.	Até amanhã.	*Ahteh ahmahnyah~.*
Sleep well.	Durma bem.	*Doormah bayn~.*
Have a very nice holiday.	Tenha umas boas férias.	*Tenyah oomahsh boahsh fehreeahsh.*

21

What you might hear

Tudo bem.	Okay.
Mais ou menos.	Okay, not too bad.
Nada mau / mal.	Not too bad.
Vai-se andando.	Life goes on.
Pois.	Yes. / I see. / Okay.
Com licença.	Excuse me.

3 - ASKING THE WAY

Useful related topics in the vocabulary section: Public transport (13).

Where is the Cathedral?	Onde é a Sé?	*Onde eh ah Sseh?*
Where is the nearest shopping centre?	Onde é o centro comercial mais próximo?	*Onde eh oo ssentroo komersseeahl mahysh prosseemoo?*

How do I get to ... street?	Como é que se vai à rua ...?	*Komoo eh ke sse vay ah rrooah ... ?*
Is this the way to the Castle?	O Castelo é por aqui?	*Oo Kahshteloo eh por ahkee?*
How long would it take to walk to the park?	Quanto tempo é que leva para ir a pé ao parque?	*Kwahntoo tempoo eh ke levah pahrah eer ah peh aho pahrk'e?*
Is there a bus that goes to the main square?	Há algum autocarro que vá para a praça principal?	*Ah ahlgoon~ aootookahroo ke vah pahrah ah prahssah preensseepahl?*
I'm looking for the parish church.	Estou à procura da igreja matriz.	*Eshtoh ah prokoorah dah eegrejah mahtreesh.*
I'm afraid I'm lost.	Peço desculpa, estou perdido / perdida.	*Pesso deshkoolpah, eshtoh perdeedoo / perdeedah.*

2

| Can you show me on the map? | Pode-me indicar no mapa? | *Pode-me eendeekahr noo mahpah?* |

What you might hear

Sempre em frente.	Go straight ahead.
Tem que dar a volta.	You have to turn around.
À direita.	To the right.
À esquerda.	To the left.
Tome a primeira à direita / a segunda à esquerda.	Take the first on the right / the second on the left.
Tem que ir até à rotunda.	You have to go to the roundabout.
Tem que atravessar a ponte.	You have to cross the bridge.

4 - MOTORING

There is a national automobile association (the ACP – *Automóvel Clube de Portugal*). If you are driving in Portugal, it would be worth while contacting them to find out what services they can offer. Most of the service stations have shops where you can buy maps and car or bike accessories. There are car rental points at the country's international airports. Motorways (*auto-estradas*) with tolls (*portagens*), connect most major towns and cities, and there are reasonable trunk roads (known as IPs and ICs) serving smaller locations. A standard British driving licence is sufficient.

Speed restrictions are as follows:

Motorways: 75 Miles/h (120 Km/h)
Major roads between towns (IPs and ICs): 56 Miles/h (100 Km/h)
Built-up areas: 30 Miles/h (50 Km/h)

Useful related topics in the vocabulary section: Motoring (10): personal details (12); telling the time (18); the weather (20).

Where can I hire a car?	Onde posso alugar um carro?	Onde posso aloogahr um~ karroo?
I'd like a small / large car	Queria um carro pequeno / grande.	Kereeah oon~ kahrroo pekenoo / grahnd'e.
What is the rate per day?	Qual é a tarifa diária?	*Kwahl eh ah tahreefah deeahreeah?*
Does the cost include petrol?	O preço inclui gasolina?	*Oo pressoo enclooee gahzoleenah?*
I'd like an automatic.	Queria um carro automático.	*Kereeah oon~ kahrroo ahootomahteekoo.*
Where can I return the car?	Onde posso devolver o carro?	*Onde possoo devolver o kahrroo?*
What insurance cover do I get?	Qual o tipo de seguro que vou ter?	*Kwahl o teepoo de ssegooroo ke voh ter?*
Can you let me have a road map?	Pode dar-me um mapa das estradas?	*Pod'e dahr-me oon~ mahpah dahsh estrahdahsh?*

| Is there a cheaper rate for a week / month? | Há alguma tarifa mais barata para o aluguer durante uma semana? / um mês? | *Ah ahlgoomah tahreefah mahysh bahrahtah pahrah o ahlooguer doorahnte oomah ssemahnah? / oon~ mesh?* |

2

On the road

I need fuel / oil / water.	Preciso de gasolina / óleo / água.	*Presseezoo de gahzoleenah / oleeoo / ahgwah.*
Fill it up.	Encher.	*Ensher*
I'd like 10 / 20 litres.	Eu queria 10 / 20 litros.	*Eyou kereeah desh / veent'e leetroosh.*
Can I check the tyres here?	Posso verificar os pneus aqui?	*Possoo vereefeekahr oosh pneyoosh ahkee?*
Where is the nearest garage?	Onde é a garagem mais próxima?	*Onde eh ah gahrahjayn~ mahysh prosseemah?*

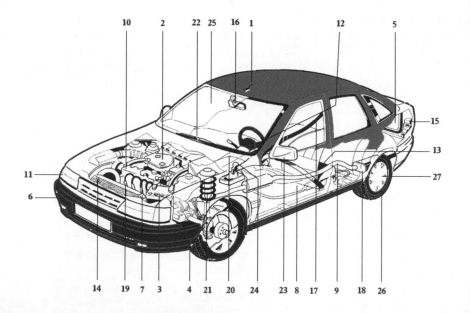

THE PARTS OF A CAR

1	aerial	*antena*
2	air filter	*filtro do ar*
3	battery	*bateria*
4	brake disk	*disco do travão*
5	boot	*mala*
6	bumper	*pára-choques*
7	distributor cables	*cabos condutores*
8	door	*porta*
9	exhaust pipe	*tubo de escape*
10	engine block	*motor*
11	headlight	*farol da frente*
12	indicator	*pisca-pisca*
13	petrol tank	*depósito de gasolina*
14	radiator	*radiador*
15	rear light	*mínimos*
16	rear-view mirror	*espelho retrovisor*
17	seat belt	*cinto de segurança*
18	silencer	*silenciador*
19	spark plug	*vela*
20	steering column	*caixa de direcção*
21	shock absorbers	*amortecedores*
22	windscreen wiper	*limpa pára-brisas*
23	wing mirror	*espelho exterior*
24	windscreen wash	*depósito de água*
25	windscreen	*pára-brisas*
26	tyre	*pneu*
27	wheel	*roda*

2

Where is the nearest petrol station?	Onde é a estação de serviço mais próxima?	*Onde eh ah eshtahssaw~ de sserveesso mahysh prosseemah?*
Is there a good road to ...?	Há alguma boa estrada para …?	*Ah ahlgoomah boah estrahdah pahrah …?*
How long will it take to drive to ...?	Quanto tempo demora até …?	*Kwahntoo tempoo demorah ahteh …?*
Can you fix the ... ?	Pode arranjar o / a …?	*Pod'e ahrrahnjahr oo / ah …?*
How long will it take?	Quanto tempo demora?	*Kwahntoo tempoo demorah?*
There is something wrong with the engine	O motor está com algum problema.	*O motor eshtah kon~ ahlgoon~ problemah.*
Is there any ... agent in this town / near here?	Há algum agente da marca … nesta cidade / aqui perto?	*Ah ahlgoon~ ahjente dah mahrkah … neshtah sseedahd'e / ahkee pertoo?*

The brakes are binding.	Os travões estão a gripar.	*Oos trahvoyn~sh eshtaw~ ah greepahr.*
The engine is overheating.	O motor está a aquecer demais.	*Oo motor eshtah ah ahkesser demahysh.*
Where can I park?	Onde posso estacionar?	*Onde possoo eshtahsseeonahr?*
I need a new tyre.	Preciso de um pneu novo.	*Presseesoo de oon~ pneyoo novoo.*
Is there a car accessory shop near here?	Há alguma loja de acessórios para carros aqui perto?	*Ah ahlgoomah lojah de ahssessoreeoos pahrah kahrroosh ahkee pertoo?*
Is this a parking meter zone?	Esta zona tem parquímetros?	*Eshtah zonah tayn~ pahrkeemetroos?*
From what time is parking free?	A partir de que horas o parqueamento é grátis?	*A pahrteer de ke orahsh oo pahrkeeahmentoo eh grateesh?*

2

31

Is there a limit to parking time?	Há algum limite de tempo para parqueamento?	*Ah ahlgoon~ leemeet'e de tempoo pahrah pahrkeeahmentoo?*

What you might hear (if you have problems with a car or caravan)

Vai levar algum tempo.	It'll take some time.
Só posso começar amanhã.	I can only start tomorrow.
Vai ser bastante caro.	It's going to be expensive.
Tem que deixar o carro.	You'll have to leave the car.

5 - BUSES, TAXIS, TRAMS AND UNDERGROUND

There are taxi services at all airports, railway and coach stations, with metered service into the local town. In-city bus services are reasonable and Lisbon has a small tram network serving the historical area of the city centre. There are good coach services across the country and practically all of the companies (public and private) have web sites where you can get up-to-date information on their services. Timetables can usually be trusted, with due allowance for traffic conditions.

Useful related topics in the vocabulary section: Numbers (11); public transport (13); telling the time (18)

Where can I get a taxi?	Onde posso apanhar um táxi?	*Onde possoo ahpahnyahr oon~ tahksee?*
What bus do I catch to...?	Qual é o autocarro que apanho para ...?	*Kwahl eh oo ahootokahrroo ke ahpahnyoo pahrah ...?*
Where is the nearest bus stop/underground station?	Onde é a paragem de autocarros/estação de metro mais perto?	*Onde eh ah pahrahjayn~ de ahootokahrroos/ah eshtahssaw~ doo metroo mahysh pertoo?*

33

What time is the next bus to ...?	A que horas é o próximo autocarro para ...?	*A ke orahsh eh oo prosseemoo ahootokahr-roo pahrah ...?*
Can you tell me when we get to ...?	Pode dizer-me quando chegamos a ...?	*Pod'e deezer-me kwahndoo shegahmoos ah ...?*
Do I get off here for ...?	Saio aqui para ...?	*Ssahyoo ahkee pahrah ...?*
Is it very far / long to ...?	É muito longe para ...?	*Eh mooeentoo lonje pahrah ...?*
I / we want to go to ... ?	Quero / Queremos ir para ...	*Keroo / Kerehmoosh eer pahrah ...?*
Does this bus go to / near ...?	Este autocarro vai para ...? /passa perto de ...?	*Eshte ahootokahrroo vahy pahrah ...? / pahssah pertoo de ...?*
Do you mind if I open / close the window?	Posso abrir / fechar a janela?	*Possoo ahbreer / feshahr ah jahnelah?*

2

How much is the ticket?	Quanto custa o bilhete?	*Kwahntoo koostah o beelyet'e?*
Where can I buy a book of tickets?	Onde é que posso comprar uma caderneta de bilhetes?	*Onde eh ke possoo komprahr oomah kahdernetah de beelyet'sh?*
Could you help me get a ticket?	Pode ajudar-me a comprar um bilhete?	*Pod'e ahjoodahr-me uh komprahr oon~ beelyet'e?*
When does the last bus / underground go?	A que horas é o último autocarro / o último metro?	*Ah ke orahsh eh o oolteemoo ahootokahrroo / ... ou oolteemoo metroo?*
Is there a night-time service to ...?	Há algum serviço nocturno para ...?	*Ah ahlgoon~ sserveessoo noktoornoo pahrah ...?*
Where do I get a tram to ...?	Onde é que posso apanhar um eléctrico para ...?	*Onde eh ke possoo ahpahnyahr oon~ elehktreekoo pahrah ...?*

6 - TAKING A TRAIN

There are inter-city rail services (*Intercidades*), run by Portuguese railways (CP),
including a very good Lisbon – Oporto intercity express (the Alfa service). Smaller
places are reasonably well connected, but timetables need to be checked and in out-of-
the-way places and it can be a long way from the station to the centre of the local town
or village. Fares are relatively low and the train is a good way to see the country. You
must buy your ticket before getting on a train - and give yourself plenty of time for this.

Useful related topics in the vocabulary section: Numbers (11); public transport (13);
telling the time (18).

At what station do I get a train to ...?	Em que estação posso apanhar um comboio para …?	*Ayn~ ke eshtahssaw~ possoo ahpahnyahr oon~ komboyoo pahrah …?*
How do I get to ... (station)?	Como é que posso ir para a estação …?	*Komoo eh ke possoo eer pahrah ah eshtahssaw~ …?*
When does the train for ... leave?	A que horas parte o comboio para …?	*Ah ke orahsh pahrt'e o komboyoo pahrah …?*

When does the train from ... arrive?	A que horas chega o comboio vindo de ...?	*Ah ke orahsh shegah o komboyoo veendoo de ...?*
When is the first / last train to ...?	A que horas é o primeiro / o último comboio para ...?	*Ah ke orahsh eh oo preemayroo / oo oolteemoo komboyoo pahrah ...?*
How much is a ticket to ...?	Quanto custa o bilhete para ...?	*Kwahntoo kooshtah oo beelyet'e pahrah ...?*
Does the train stop at ...?	O comboio pára em ...?	*O komboyoo pahrah ayn~ ...?*
What stop do I get off for ...?	Em que paragem saio para ...?	*Ayn~ ke pahrahjayn~ ssahyoo pahrah ...?*
How long does it take to get to ...?	Quanto tempo demora até ...?	*Kwahntoo tempoo demorah ahteh ...?*
I'd like a single / return ticket to...	Quero um bilhete simples / um bilhete de ida e volta para ...	*Keroo oon~ beelyet'e seemplesh / oon~ beelyet'e de eedah e voltah pahrah ...*

2

English	Portuguese	Pronunciation
I'd like to reserve a seat.	Gostaria de reservar um lugar.	*Goshtahreeah de rezervahr oon~ loogahr.*
Is this the right platform for the train to ...?	É esta a plataforma do comboio para …?	*Eh eshtah ah plahtahformah doo komboyoo pahrah …?*
Which platform is for ...?	Qual é a plataforma para …?	*Kwahl eh ah plahtahformah pahrah …?*
Is the train on time?	O comboio sai no horário?	*Oo komboyoo ssahy noo orahreeoo?*
Could you help me with my luggage?	Pode ajudar-me com a bagagem?	*Pod'e ahjoodahr-me kom ah bahgahjayn~?*
Where can I get a porter?	Onde posso arranjar um bagageiro?	*Onde possoo ahrrahnjahr oon~ bahgahjayroo?*
Is this seat free?	Este lugar está livre?	*Eshte loogahr eshtah leevr'e?*
What time do we arrive in ...?	A que horas chegamos a …?	*Ah ke orahsh shegahmoos ah …?*

| How long do we stop here? | Quanto tempo ficamos aqui parados? | *Kwahntoo tempoo feekah-moos ahkee pahrahdoos?* |
| Does the train stop at ...? | O comboio pára em ...? | *O komboyoo parah ayn~ ...?* |

2

What you might see

Bilheteira	Ticket Office
Informações	Information
Partidas	Departures
Chegadas	Arrivals
Vagão restaurante	Restaurant car
Pare, escute e olhe	Stop, listen and watch

7 - AT THE HOTEL

There is a wide range of hotels, based on a 5-star system, with the best offering luxury accommodation. You will also find the terms *estalagem* (luxury inn), *pousada* (high quality inn, often in an area of outstanding natural beauty or in a building of historic interest), *residêncial* (boarding house) and *pensão* (cheap hotel, found near railway stations and in the centre of most reasonably-sized towns).

Useful related topics in the vocabulary section: Days and months (6), hotels (9).

Do you have a single room?	Tem algum quarto individual?	*Tayn~ ahlgoon~ kwahrtoo eendeeveedooahl?*
I'm / We're staying for one night.	Vou / vamos ficar uma noite.	*Voh / vahmoos feekahr oomah noyt'e.*
I'd like a room for one week.	Queria um quarto para uma semana.	*Kereeah oon~ kwahrtoo pahrah oomah ssemahnah.*
Can you give me a morning call?	Pode acordar-me de manhã?	*Pod'e ahkordahr-me de mahnyah?*

40

2

How much is a double room?	Quanto custa um quarto de casal?	*Kwahntoo kooshtah oon~ kwahrtoo de kahzahl?*
Can we have an extra bed?	Podemos ter uma cama extra?	*Podehmoosh ter oomah kahmah ehshtrah?*
Do you serve breakfast?	Servem o pequeno almoço?	*Sservayn~ oo pekenoo ahlmossoo?*
What time do you serve lunch / dinner?	A que horas servem o almoço / jantar?	*Ah ke orahsh servayn~ oo ahlmossoo / jahntahr?*
Is there a public phone I can use?	Há algum telefone público que eu possa usar?	*Ah ahlgoon~ telefone poobleekoo ke eyoo possah oozahr?*
Can I e-mail from the hotel?	Posso enviar e-mails do hotel?	*Possoo enveeahr ee-mahyls doo otel?*
Can I receive e-mails during my stay?	Posso receber e-mails durante a minha estadia?	*Possoo rresseber ee-mahyls doorahnte ah meenyah eshtahdeeah?*

I'd like a room which is not facing the street.	Queria um quarto que não seja virado para a rua.	*Kereeah oon~ kwahrto ke naw~ ssayjah veerahdo pahrah ah rrooah.*
Could I see the room?	Posso ver o quarto?	*Possoo ver oo kwahrtoo?*
Do you have a larger / smaller room?	Tem algum quarto maior / mais pequeno?	*Tayn~ ahlgoon~ kwahrtoo mahyor / mahysh pekenoo?*
Do you have a less expensive room?	Tem algum quarto mais barato?	*Tayn~ ahlgoon~ kwahrtoo mahysh bahrahtoo?*
Can I put this in the hotel safe?	Posso deixar isto no cofre?	*Possoo dayshahr eeshtoo noo kofr'e?*
Where can I park my car safely?	Onde posso estacionar o carro em segurança?	*Onde possoo eshtahsseeonahr oo kahrroo ayn~ ssegoorahnssah?*
Does the hotel have a garage?	O hotel tem garagem?	*Oo otel tayn~ gahrahjayn~?*

What you might hear:

Quanto tempo quer ficar?	How long do you want to stay?
Identificação por favor.	Your I.D. please.
A garagem é atrás do hotel.	The garage is at the back of the hotel.

8 - CAMPING

There are campsites all along the Portuguese coastline, especially near the most popular resorts. An international Campers' Card is useful and in the high season a phone call to the site is essential if you are arriving in the evening, both to check on closing times and on the availability of a site for your tent or caravan.

Useful related topics in the vocabulary section: Camping (3); personal details (12); telling the time (18); the weather (20).

How far is the nearest campsite?	Onde é que fica o parque de campismo mais próximo?	*Onde eh ke feekah oo pahrke de kahmpeeshmo mahysh prosseemoo?*
How much is it per night?	Quanto custa por noite?	*Kwahnto kooshtah por noyt'e?*
What time does it close?	A que horas fecha?	*Ah ke orahsh fehshah?*
Can I book by phone?	Posso reservar pelo telefone?	*Possoo rezervahr pelo telefon'e?*
Is there drinking water?	Há água potável no parque?	*Ah ahgwah potahvel noo pahrk'e?*
Are there any showers / washing machines / cooking facilities on site?	Há duches / máquinas de lavar / equipamento para cozinhar no parque?	*Ah dooshes / mahkeenahsh de lahvahr / ekeepahmento pahrah kozeenyahr noo pahrk'e?*

2

Can you help me put up the tent?	Pode ajudar-me a montar a tenda?	*Pod'e ahjoodahr-me ah montahr ah tendah?*
Can we bring a pet?	Podemos trazer um animal de estimação?	*Podehmoosh trahzer oon~ ahneemahl de esteemahssaw~?*
Can we choose our own site?	Podemos escolher o nosso lugar?	*Podehmoosh eskolyer oo nossoo loogahr?*
We'd like a quiet site.	Queríamos um lugar tranquilo.	*Kereeahmoosh oon~ loogahr trahnkeeloo.*
Can we park the car next to the tent / caravan?	Podemos estacionar o carro junto à tenda / caravana?	*Podehmoosh eshtahsseeonahr oo kahrroo joontoo ah tendah/ kahrahvahnah?*
We'd like to stay for one night / a week.	Queríamos ficar uma noite / uma semana.	*Kerehmoosh feekahr oomah noyt'e / oomah ssemahnah.*

45

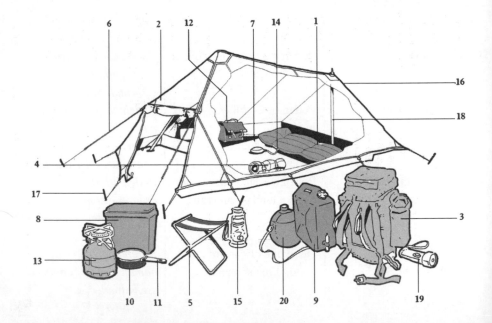

CAMPING EQUIPMENT

1	airbed	*cama insuflável*		12	pannier	*saco para bicicleta*
2	awning	*toldo*		13	primus stove	*fogão de campismo*
3	backpack	*mochila*		14	pump	*bomba de ar*
4	carry mat	*tapete*		15	storm lantern	*lanterna*
5	folding chair	*cadeira dobrável*		16	tent	*tenda*
6	guy rope	*espia*		17	tent peg	*cavilha*
7	groundsheet	*oleado*		18	tent pole	*estaca da tenda*
8	insulated picnic box	*geladeira*		19	torch	*lanterna de bolso*
9	jerry can	*lata*		20	water bottle	*cantil*
10	pan	*panela*				
11	pan handle	*pega da panela*				

2

Do you sell butane / propane gas?	Vende gás butano / propano?	*Vend'e gahsh bootahnoo / propahnoo?*
Can we have our own barbecue?	Podemos fazer um churrasco?	*Podehmoosh fahzer oon~ shoorrahshko?*
Is there a play area for children?	Há algum lugar para as crianças brincarem no parque?	*Ah ahlgoon~ loogahr pahrah ahsh kreeahnssahsh breen~kahrayn~ noo pahrk'e?*

9 - GETTING TO KNOW PEOPLE

This section is a follow-up to section 2 and is aimed at visitors staying for some time in one place rather than travelling around for their holiday. The last part focuses on a more specific relationship and a major health concern.

Useful related topics in the vocabulary section: Days of the week, months, seasons and special dates (6); personal details (12).

Also see the examples of language functions in the grammar section.

What would you like to do today / this evening?	O que gostaria de fazer hoje? / esta noite?	*Oo ke gostahreeah de fahzer oj'e? / eshtah noyt'e?*
I'd like to go to ... / visit ...	Gostaria de ir ... / visitar ...?	*Gostahreeah de eer ... / veezeetahr ...?*
Can we meet again?	Podemos encontrar-nos outra vez?	*Podehmoosh enkontrahr-noos ohtrah vesh?*
Is there a magazine showing what's on?	Há alguma revista com os programas na cidade?	*Ah ahlgoomah reveeshtah kom oosh prograhmahsh nah sseedahd'e?*
Where can I find out about ...?	Onde posso encontrar pormenores sobre ...?	*Onde possoo enkontrahr pormenoresh ssobr'e ...?*
We're having a wonderful time.	Estamos a divertir-nos imenso.	*Eshtahmoosh ah deeverteer-noos eemensoo.*

2

49

Do you have any hobbies?	Tem algum passatempo preferido?	*Tayn~ ahlgoon~ pahssahtempoo preferee doo?*
I like painting / playing the guitar / piano.	Gosto de pintar / tocar guitarra / piano.	*Goshto de peentahr / tokahr gueetahrrah / peeahnoo.*
I think I'm falling in love with you.	Acho que estou a apaixonar-me por ti.	*Ahshoo ke eshtoh ah apaysheeonahr-me por tee.*
Will you stay with me tonight?	Ficas comigo hoje à noite?	*Feekash comeegoo oj'e ah noyt'e?*
I'll only go as far as you want to.	Só vou até onde quiseres.	*Ssoh voh ahteh onde keezer'sh.*
I always use a condom.	Uso sempre o preservativo.	*Oozoo ssempr'e oo prezer vahteevoo.*
Are you worried about AIDS?	Estás preocupado (a) com a SIDA?	*Eshtash preeocoopahdoo (ah) con~ ah sseedah?*

What you might hear

2

Já tenho namorado / namorada.	I've already got a boyfriend / girlfriend.
Preciso de mais tempo.	I need more time.
Não podemos correr riscos.	We mustn't take any risks.
Não estou preparado/a para isso.	I'm not prepared to do that.
Prefiro falar mais sobre o assunto amanhã.	I'd rather talk more about this tomorrow.
Ainda não nos conhecemos bem.	We don't know each other well enough yet.

10 - SHOPPING

The usual opening hours for local shops are 9 am to 1 pm and 3 pm to 7 pm. There are bigger supermarkets which are open until 8 pm or 9 pm and shops in malls (known as *Centros comerciais)* are often open until 10 pm or midnight. Out-of-town superstores are known as *hipermarchés.*

If you are shopping for clothes or shoes, use the conversion tables (Section 5). Ask for a receipt (*recibo*) in case you need to take something back.

You can buy local produce from the market (*mercado*) as well as in small grocers (*mercearias*) or supermarkets. It is worth finding out where the best local market is and going there in the early morning if you want to try some of the wide variety of fish that is caught around the coast of Portugal. For specific fish, see the section on restaurants and cafés.

Useful related topics in the vocabulary section: Clothing (4); numbers (11); shopping (15). See also Section 5 (Conversion tables).

2

Where can I buy ...?	Onde posso comprar ...?	*Onde possoo komprahr ...?*
When does this shop open?	A que horas abre esta loja?	*A ke orahsh ahbr'e eshtah lojah?*
Where is the clothing department?	Onde é a secção de roupa?	*Onde eh ah ssekssaw~ de rohpah?*
Could you help me?	Pode ajudar-me?	*Pod'e ahjoodahr-me?*
I'm looking for ...	Estou à procura de ...?	*Eshtoh ah prokoorah de ...?*
Do you sell English-language newspapers?	Vende jornais de língua inglesa?	*Vend'e jornahysh de leengwah eenglezah?*
I'm just looking.	Estou só a ver.	*Eshtoh ssoh ah ver.*
Can I look around the shop?	Posso dar uma vista de olhos pela loja?	*Possoo dahr oomah veeshtah de olyosh pelah lojah?*

53

Could you show me a/some ... ?	Podia mostrar-me um ... / alguns …?	*Podeeah mooshtrahr-me oon~ ... / ahlgoon~sh …?*
This is not quite what I want.	Não é bem o que eu queria.	*Naw~ eh bayn~ oo ke eyoo kereeah.*
Do you have something cheaper / smaller?	Tem alguma coisa mais barata / pequena?	*Tayn~ ahlgoomah koyzah mahysh bahrahtah / pekenah?*
I'll take this one.	Levo este / esta.	*Levoo esht'e / eshtah.*
I'm afraid it's too expensive.	É muito caro / cara.	*Eh mooeentoo kahroo / kahrah.*
I haven't got enough money on me.	Não tenho dinheiro suficiente comigo.	*Naw~ tenyo deenyayroo ssoofeessee-ente komeego.*
Can you keep this for me?	Pode guardar isto para mim?	*Pod'e gwahrdahr eeshtoo pahrah mee?*
Could you gift-wrap this for me?	Podia embrulhar para oferta?	*Podeeah embroolyahr pahrah ofertah?*

54

11 - IN A BANK

Banks are open from 8:30 am to 3:00 pm and provide all the services you would expect. There is a very good ATM service, especially in the bigger towns. Look for the *Multibanco* sign. You can transfer money through the Post Office and the banks, though if you are sending money it is a good idea to check various banks because rates vary considerably. There are also specialist agents who carry out exchange operations, especially in Lisbon and Oporto. Banks at airports are also good for currency operations.

Useful related topics in the vocabulary section: Numbers (11); personal details (12).

Where can I find a bank?	Onde posso encontrar um banco?	*Onde possoo enkontrahr oon~ bahnkoo?*
Can I get money on my credit card?	Posso levantar dinheiro com o meu cartão de crédito?	*Possoo levahntahr deenyayroo kom o meyoo kahrtaw~ de crehdeetoo?*
What's the maximum per day?	Qual é o máximo por dia?	*Kwahl eh oo masseemoo por deeah?*

I've had some money transferred here.	Mandei transferir algum dinheiro para este banco.	*Mahnday trahnsfereer ahlgoon~ deenyayroo pahrah eshte bahnkoo.*
These are the details of my bank.	Estes são os pormenores do meu banco.	*Eshtes ssaw~ oosh pormenooresh do meyoo bahnkoo.*
What's the exchange rate? I'd like to change this into euros. Could you give me some small change?	Qual é o câmbio? Gostaria de trocar isto em euros. Pode dar-me algum dinheiro em notas de pequeno valor?	*Kwahl eh oo cambeeoo? Gostahreeah de trokahr eestoo ayn~ eyoorosh. Pod'e dahr-me ahlgoon~ deenyaroo ayn~ notahsh de pekenoo vahlor?*

What you might hear

2

Posso ver alguma identificação?	Can I see some ID ?
É favor preencher este formulário.	Please fill in this form.
Pode voltar amanhã?	Can you come back tomorrow?
Pode assinar aqui?	Can you sign here?
O seu cartão não foi aceite.	Your card wasn't accepted.

12 - IN A RESTAURANT OR CAFÉ

The Portuguese are very proud of the wide variety of their cooking both national and regional, and there is a separate section (entitled **SOME TYPICAL PORTUGUESE**

57

DISHES) where a description of some of the most popular dishes will be found. It is usual to leave a tip after a meal but there is no set percentage. A lot of cooking is done in olive oil and with garlic. For translations of fish, meat and shellfish, see the end of this section. Apart from the standard word *restaurante*, you will find *café-bar, churrasqueira* (a restaurant specialising in barbecued dishes), *esplanada* (pavement café), *snack-bar* (a small restaurant serving soups, sandwiches and a selection of meals of the day - *pratos do dia*) and *pastelaria* (cake shop). The Portuguese themselves often have a favourite local restaurant which they call a *tasca*. In many of these you can find very good home cooking and reasonably priced wines. Wines are divided into three types: demarcated regions (D.O.C.), higher quality regional wines (V.Q.P.R.D.) and ordinary table wines. There are good red and white wines, and also the special Portuguese *vinho verde* (green wine) which is very young, sparkling wine, available in white and red. The red is very much an acquired taste.

All restaurants and coffee shops must have a complaints book available and display a notice to this effect.

Useful related topics in the vocabulary section: Cafés and restaurants (2); days of the week (6); numbers (11); telling the time (18).

2

We'd like to have lunch/dinner.	Gostaríamos de almoçar / jantar.	*Gostahreeahmoosh de ahlmossahr / jahntahr.*
We'd like a quick meal.	Tem refeições rápidas?	*Tayn~ refayssoyn~sh rahpeedahsh?*
We'd like to have a drink first.	Gostaríamos de tomar uma bebida antes.	*Goshtahreeahmoosh de tomahr oomah bebeedah ahntesh.*
Can I see the menu?	Posso ver a ementa?	*Possoo ver ah ementah?*
Can I see the wine list?	Posso ver a carta de vinhos?	*Possoo ver ah kahrtah de veenyoosh?*
Do you have a menu in English?	Tem a ementa em inglês?	*Tayn~ ah ementah ayn~ eenglesh?*
Do you have a dish of the day?	Tem prato do dia?	*Tayn~ prahtoo doo deeah?*

We haven't decided yet.	Ainda não decidimos.	*Aheendah naw~ desseedeemoosh.*
What would you recommend?	O que nos recomenda?	*Oo ke noosh rekomendah?*
What are the specialities of the region?	Quais são as especialidades da região?	*Kwahysh ssaw~ ahsh eshpesseeahleedahdesh dah rejeeaw~?*
Do you have any wines from this region?	Tem alguns vinhos desta região?	*Tayn~ ahlgoons veenyos deshtah rejeeaw~?*
Can we have something to start with?	Pode dar-nos algo para entrada?	*Pod'e dahr-noos ahlgoo pahrah entrahdah?*
How long is the meal going to take?	Quanto tempo demora este prato?	*Kwahnto tempo demorah este prahto?*
I'm a vegetarian.	Sou vegetariano.	*Ssoh vejetahreeahnoo.*

Can I have a plain omelette.	Pode-me servir uma omolete simples.	*Pod'e-me sserveer oon~ omelet'e sseemplesh?*
I'd like a plain salad / a salad without salt / without olive oil.	Queria uma salada sem tempero / sem sal / sem azeite.	*Kereeah oomah ssahlahdah ssayn~ tempero / ssayn~ ssahl / ssayn~ ahzayt'e.*
We've been waiting for 20 minutes.	Já estamos aqui há vinte minutos à espera.	*Jah eshtahmoosh ahkee ah veent'e meenootoosh ah eshperah.*
Is there garlic in this dish?	Este prato contém alho?	*Eshte prahtoo kontayn~ ahlyoo?*
The food was very good.	A comida estava muito boa.	*Ah komeedah eshtahvah mooeento boah.*
A coffee, please.	Um café / uma bica, por favor.	*Oon~ kahfeh / oomah beekah, por fahvor.*
Do you have any sweeteners?	Tem adoçante?	*Tayn~ ahdossahnt'e?*

2

In the evening, what time do you stop cooking?	A que horas fecha a cozinha à noite?	*Ah ke orahsh feshah ah kozeenyah ah noyt'e?*
Do you have any alcohol-free beer?	Tem alguma cerveja sem álcool?	*Tayn~ ahlgoomah sservejah ssayn~ ahlkol?*
I'd like a soft drink.	Queria uma bebida sem álcool.	*Kereeah oomah bebeedah ssayn~ ahlkool.*
Can I have the bill, please?	Pode trazer-me a conta, por favor?	*Pod'e trahzer-me ah kontah, por fahvor?*
This isn't what I ordered.	Não pedi isto.	*Naw~ pedee eeshtoo.*
Can you explain the bill?	Pode explicar-me a conta?	*Pod'e eshpleekahr-me ah kontah?*
I'd like to see the manager.	Gostaria de falar com o gerente.	*Gostahreeah de fahlahr kom oo jerent'e.*
This wine is not good.	Este vinho não está bom.	*Eshte veenyoo naw~ eshtah bon~.*
The food is very salty.	A comida está muito salgada.	*Ah komeedah eshtah mooeentoo ssahlgahdah.*

62

Where are the toilets?	Onde é a casa de banho?	*Onde eh ah kahzah de bahnyoo?*
The toilet is locked.	A casa de banho está fechada à chave.	*Ah kahzah de bahnyoo eshtah feshahdah ah shahv'e.*
There's no toilet paper in the bathroom.	Não há papel higiénico na casa de banho.	*Naw~ ah pahpel eejee-ehneekoo nah kahzah de bahnyoo.*
Can I have the complaints book?	Traga-me o livro de reclamações.	*Trahgah-me oo leevroo de reclahmahssoyn~sh.*
The main course was very good but ...	O prato principal estava muito bom, mas …	*Oo prahtoo preensseepahl eshtahvah mooeentoo bom, mahsh …*
We won't come back here.	Não voltamos aqui.	*Naw~ voltahmoosh ahkee.*

What you might hear

Quer / Deseja mais alguma coisa?	Is there anything else you would like?
Quer / Querem algo para petiscar / para entrada?	Would you like a starter of some kind?
E para beber?	What would you like to drink?
Água com gás ou sem gás?	Plain or sparkling water?
Fresco ou natural?	Chilled or room temperature?

What you might see

Fechado	Closed
Descanso do pessoal	Staff day off
Existe Livro de Reclamações	Complaints Book available

What you might see in a restaurant

Fish

atum - tuna fish
bacalhau - cod
caldeirada - fish stew
carapau - horse-mackerel
cherne - turbot
enguia - eel

garoupa - sea perch
linguado - sole
pargo - bream
peixe espada - scabbard fish
pescada - whiting

robalo - sea bass
salmão - salmon
sarda - mackerel
sardinha - sardine
truta - trout

Meat

bife - steak
borrego - lamb
coelho - rabbit
frango - chicken

fígado - liver
pato - duck
perú - turkey

porco - pork
rim - kidney
vitela - veal

65

Sea food

ameijoa - clam	gamba - prawn	lula - squid
camarão - shrimp	lagosta - lobster	marisco - shell fish
carangueijo - crab	lampreia - lamprey	polvo - octopus
choco - cuttle-fish		

Ways of cooking

caril - curry	estufado - braised	molho - sauce
cozido - boiled	grelhado - grilled	recheado - stuffed
ensopado - stewed		

13 – KEEPING IN TOUCH: POSTAL AND TELEPHONE SERVICES

2

Look for signs saying *Correios* (Post Office) or *CTT*. Stamps can be also be bought in hotels and on some camp sites. There is a two-tier service (*correio azul* being the faster). You can telephone from most post offices and there is usually a special counter (*Telefone*) where you ask for a line, make your call and then pay the charge. A reverse charge call is *Chamada paga no destino*. See the section on useful phone numbers (p 147).

There is a Netpost system available in many post offices and this enables you to make phone calls and to get Internet access for a fee paid at the counter.

For those interested in collecting recent Portuguese stamps, there is a philatelist department in the main Post Office in Lisbon (in the *Restauradores* square).

In some post offices there is a ticket system (*senhas*) and you should take a ticket straight away and keep track of the numbers as they come up on the information board.

The *Poste Restante* system is also available in many Post Offices across the country.

Useful related topics in the vocabulary section: Countries (5); numbers (11); personal details (12); sending mail and communicating (14); time phrases (19).

Where's the post office?	Onde é a estação dos Correios?	*Onde eh ah eshtahssaw~ doosh korrayoosh?*
Is there a postbox near here?	Há alguma caixa dos Correios aqui próximo?	*Ah ahlgoomah kahyshah doos korrayoos ahkee prosseemoo?*
How much is a letter / postcard to ... ?	Quanto é uma carta / um bilhete postal para …?	*Kwahntoo eh oomah kahrtah / oon~ beelyete postahl pahrah …?*
Is there any mail for me?	Há correio para mim?	*A korrayoo pahrah mee?*
I'd like this to be sent first class mail.	Gostaria de enviar isto por correio azul.	*Gostahreeah de enveeahr eeshtoo por korrayo ahzool.*
Do you have an internet connection?	Tem ligação por internet?	*Tayn~ leegahssaw~ por eenternet?*
Can I phone from here?	Posso telefonar daqui?	*Possoo telefonahr dahkee?*

I'd like to make a reverse charge call.	Gostaria de fazer uma chamada paga no destino.	*Gostahreeah de fahzer ooma shahmahdah pahgah noo deshteenoo.*
What is the code for ...?	Qual é o código para ...?	*Kwahl eh oo kodeegooo pahrah ...?*
Do you have padded envelopes?	Tem envelopes almofadados?	*Tayn~ envelopes ahlmofahdahdoos?*
Do you have small boxes for parcel post?	Tem caixas pequenas para volumes?	*Tayn~ kayshahsh pekenahsh pahrah voloomesh?*

2

What you might see

Tire a senha	Take a number slip
Atendimento geral	All main services
EMS	Express mail
Registos	Registered mail
Telefone	Telephone

14 - GOING TO THE BEACH

There is a flag system at beaches, indicating whether there is a lifeguard on call.
A green flag indicates that the beach is being supervised and it is safe to swim. A yellow flag indicates that it is dangerous to swim and bathing should be restricted to short periods close to the beach. A red flag indicates that it is forbidden to swim. The lifeguard has

70

the right to stop you entering the water. A <u>chequered flag</u> indicates that there is no life-guard on duty. A <u>blue flag</u> means that the water has been subject to inspection by the EU and is considered to be clean enough for swimming.

Remember that the summer sun is very hot in Portugal and sun tan lotion with high protection levels should be used at all times. It is best to avoid exposure to the sun in the middle of the day.

It is often possible to hire a tent or awning on the beach. This will be in a *zona de concessão* and you can sit under an awning and wait for the attendant – as long as you have payment to hand. Prices are usually for full or half day but they are not unreasonable. They differ according to the popularity of the beach and the time of year.

Useful related topics in the vocabulary section: Sports (16); the weather (20).

Is there a good beach near here?	Há alguma boa praia aqui perto?	*Ah ahlgoomah boah prahyah ahkee pertoo?*

71

Is it in walking distance?	É muito longe indo a pé?	*Eh mooeentoo lonje eendoo ah peh?*
Is there a lifeguard?	Tem nadador-salvador?	*Tayn~ nahdahdor-ssahlvahdor?*
Is the water very cold?	A água é muito fria?	*Ah ahgwah eh mooeentoo freeah?*
Can I hire a beach tent / a deck-chair?	Posso alugar um toldo / uma cadeira de praia?	*Possoo ahloogahr oon~ toldoo / oomah kahdayrah de prahyah?*
Can I buy sun tan lotion on the beach?	Posso comprar protector solar na praia?	*Possoo komprahr protektor ssolahr nah prahyah?*
Can I hire a windsurf here?	Posso alugar uma prancha de windsurf aqui?	*Possoo ahloogahr oomah prahnshah de weendssoorf ahkee?*
Is it safe for children?	É seguro para as crianças?	*Eh ssegooroo pahrah ahsh kreeahnssahsh?*

What is the best time to go for a swim?	Qual é a melhor hora para tomar banho?	*Kwahl eh ah melyor orah pahrah tomahr bahnyoo?*
Can I camp on the beach?	Posso acampar na praia?	*Possoo ahkahmpahr nah prahyah?*
Where can I buy beach towels / sun tan lotion?	Onde posso comprar toalhas de praia / protector solar?	*Onde possoo komprahr tooahlyahsh de prahyah / protektor ssolahr?*
Are dogs allowed on this beach?	É permitido cães nesta praia?	*Eh permeeteedoo kayn~sh neshtah prahyah?*
Is the tide coming in or going out?	A maré está a subir ou a vazar?	*A mahreh eshtah ah ssoobeer oh ah vahzahr?*

2

What you might hear

Proibido nadar.	No swimming is allowed.
O mar está perigoso.	The sea is dangerous.
O mar está a puxar muito.	The current is pulling strongly.

15 - SPORTS

There is a wide variety of sports played in Portugal and it usually possible to buy tickets for games at any stadium on the day of the match. Prices for football matches (the most popular sport) vary according to the teams playing and the big matches can be quite expensive.

It may be possible to play a particular sport at a club and you can check in a local edition of the Yellow Pages (start with *Desportos*) to see what is available.

There are a number of places where you can indulge in extreme sports (*Desportos radicais*) and you can get details of these through the Internet. (See the note on the Portuguese postal system – Section 13 for an indication of the Internet connection they provide).

2

Useful related topics in the vocabulary section: Sports (16); the weather (20).

Is there a sports centre near here?	Há algum complexo desportivo aqui perto?	*Ah ahlgoon~ komplexoo deshporteevoo ahkee pertoo?*
What sports can I play here?	Quais são os desportos que posso praticar / jogar aqui?	*Kwahysh ssaw~ oos deshportoos ke possoo prahtee kahr / jogahr ahkee?*
Is there a swimming pool near here?	Há alguma piscina aqui perto?	*Ah ahlgoomah peesheenah ahkee pertoo?*
How much does it cost per hour / day?	Quanto custa por hora / dia?	*Kwahntoo kooshtah por orah / deeah?*

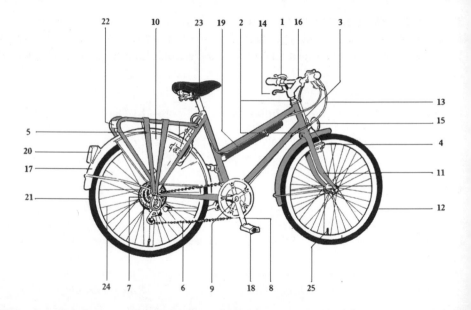

THE PARTS OF A BICYCLE

2

1	bell	*campainha*
2	bicycle fork	*caixa de esferas*
3	brake cable	*cabo de travão*
4	brake pad	*bloco de travão*
5	carrier straps	*elásticos de porta bagagem*
6	chain	*corrente*
7	chain wheel	*roda dentada*
8	crank	*alavanca de pedal*
9	crank axle	*eixo de pedal*
10	dress guard	*protector (de vestuário)*
11	fork	*forqueta*
12	front wheel	*roda da frente*
13	gear cable	*cabo de velocidades / de engrenagem*

14	gear change	*manete das velocidades*
15	headlamp	*farol*
16	handlebar	*guiador*
17	mudguard	*guarda-lamas*
18	pedal	*pedal*
19	pump	*bomba*
20	rear lamp	*luz da rectaguarda*
21	rear wheel	*pneu de trás*
22	reflector	*reflector*
23	seat	*selim*
24	spoke	*raio*
25	valve	*pipo de válvula*

How much is a round of golf?	Quanto é uma partida de golfe?	*Kwantoo eh oomah pahrteedah de golf'e?*
Do I have to book in advance?	É necessário reservar com antecedência?	*Eh nessessahreeoo rrezervahr kon~ ahntessedehsseeah?*
Can I hire a boat?	Posso alugar um barco?	*Possoo ahloogahr oon~ bahrkoo?*
Can I hire any equipment?	Posso alugar algum equipamento?	*Possoo ahloogahr ahlgoon~ ekeepahmentoo?*
Are there any fishing expeditions?	Há alguma expedição de pesca?	*Ah ahlgoomah eshpedeessaw~ de peskah?*
Are there any tennis courts?	Há algum corte de ténis aqui próximo?	*Ah ahlgoon~ kort'e de tehnees ahkee prosseemoo?*
Are there any more adventurous sports which I can play here?	Há mais desportos radicais que eu possa praticar aqui?	*Ah maysh deshportoos rahdeekahysh ke eyoo possah prahteekahr ahkee?*

16 - HEALTH

In an emergency, it is best to go straight to a local hospital rather than try to find a doctor or health centre. You can find a full list of hospitals, doctors and dentists in the Yellow Pages (*Páginas Amarelas*) of the telephone directory. Many towns have a 24-hour private house-call system, but doctors' visits are charged.

Chemists (*farmácias*) are open until 7 p.m. though they often close for lunch from 1 pm to 3 pm. There is a 24 hour service in most towns and cities: the address of the *farmácia de serviço* will be displayed in the window of all chemists but you have to pay a small fee for night-time service. At night, there is a green cross lit up outside the main door, indicating that a chemist is available.

Useful related topics in the vocabulary section: Days of the week (6); health (8); personal details (12); telephoning (17).

| Could you call a doctor? | Pode chamar um médico? | *Pod'e shahmahr oon~ mehdeekoo?* |

Can I make an appointment?	Posso marcar uma consulta?	*Possoo mahrkahr oomah konsooltah?*
When can the doctor come?	Quando é que o médico pode vir?	*Kwahndoo eh ke oo mehdeekoo pod'e veer?*
I've got an appointment for ...	Tenho uma consulta às ( ) …	*Tenyoo oomah konsooltah ahsh …*
I don't feel well.	Não me sinto bem.	*Naw~ me sseentoo bayn~.*
I feel dizzy / sick.	Sinto-me tonto (a)/ enjoado (a).	*Sseentoo-me tontoo (ah) / enjoahdoo (ah).*
I've got a bad cold.	Tenho uma grande constipação.	*Tenyoo oomah grahnd'e konshteepahssaw~.*
I think it's flu.	Penso que é uma gripe.	*Penssoo ke eh oomah greep'e.*
It hurts here.	Dói-me aqui.	*Doy-me ahkee.*
It's not usually so bad.	Não é normal ser tão forte.	*Não eh normahl sser tão fort'e.*
I've got a headache / migraine.	Tenho uma dor de cabeça / enxaqueca.	*Tenyoo oomah dor de kahbessah / enshahkekah.*

2

I'm running a temperature.	Tenho febre.	*Tenyoo febr'e.*
It may be just a hangover.	Pode ser só uma ressaca.	*Pod'e sser ssoh oomah ressahkah.*
I've been stung by a wasp / an insect / a jellyfish.	Fui picado / picada por uma vespa / um insecto / uma alforreca.	*Fooee peekahdoo / peekahdah por oomah veshpah / oon~ eensectoo / oomah ahlforrekah.*
I've been bitten by a dog.	Fui mordido/ mordida por um cão.	*Fooee mordeedoo/ mordeedah por oon~ kaw~.*
I've cut / burned myself.	Cortei-me / Queimei-me.	*Kortay-me / Kaymay-me.*
I've sprained my ankle.	Torci o tornozelo.	*Torssee o tornozeloo.*
Do I have to stay in bed?	Tenho de ficar de cama?	*Tenyoo de feekahr de kahmah?*
Can I drive if I'm taking this?	Posso conduzir se tomar este medicamento?	*Possoo kondoozeer sse tomahr eshte medeekahmentoo?*
Are there any side effects?	Tem efeitos secundários?	*Tayn~ efaytoosh ssekoondahreeoosh?*

81

Your personal medical history

My blood type is ...	O meu sangue é tipo…	*O meyoo ssahngue eh teepoo…*
I'm diabetic.	Sou diabético / diabética.	*Ssoh deeahbehteekoo / deeahbeteekah.*
I'm taking ...	Estou a tomar …	*Eshtoh ah tomahr …*
I'm allergic to ...	Sou alérgico / alérgica a …	*Ssoh ahlerjeekoo / ahlerjeekah ah …*
I'm on a special diet.	Estou a fazer uma dieta rigorosa.	*Eshtoh ah fahzer oomah dee-etah rreegorozah.*
I've already had a heart attack.	Já tive um enfarte.	*Ja teeve oon~ enfahrt'e.*
This may be my period pains.	Pode ser dores menstruais.	*Pod'e sser doresh menstrooaysh.*
I always have a heavy period.	Tenho sempre uma menstruação muito forte.	*Tenyoo ssempre oomah menstrooahssaw~ mooeentoo fort'e.*

What the doctor or chemist might say

Qual é o seu problema?	What seems to be the problem?
Há quanto tempo está assim?	How long has it been like this?
Gostaria de verificar a sua tensão arterial.	I'd like to check your blood pressure.
Deite-se aqui.	Lie down here.
Tem que fazer análises ao sangue c urina.	You must get a blood and urine test done.
Tem que fazer um raio-X.	You must get an X-ray.
Volte daqui a uma semana.	Come back in a week.
Dissolver cm água.	Dissolve this in water.
Friccionar com pomada.	Rub the ointment in.
Respire fundo.	Breathe deeply.

Tussa.	Cough.
Abra a boca.	Open your mouth.
É alérgico a alguma coisa?	Are you allergic to anything?
Está a tomar algum medicamento?	Are you on any medication?
Já foi vacinado (a) contra o tétano?	Have you had a tetanus injection?
Tem uma infecção.	You've got an infection.
Tem que ficar de cama durante ...	You must stay in bed for ...
Tem que beber muitos líquidos.	You must drink lots of liquids.
Tome dois por dia antes / depois das refeições.	Take two a day before / after meals.
Apanhou uma intoxicação alimentar.	You've got food-poisoning.
É / Não é contagioso.	It's (not) contagious

17 – IN AN EMERGENCY [1]

The number for emergencies is 112 and the three services are:

> - police: polícia *(poleesseeah)*
> - ambulance: ambulância *(ahmboolahnsseeah)*
> - fire: bombeiros *(bombayroosh)*.

The number for the forest fire service is 117.

Be ready to give your name and the number you are ringing from. Phrases from section 2 (p 18) could also be useful.

The phrases in this section are for use if you have to go to the police or to your Embassy.

---

[1] These numbers are correct at the time of printing.

Useful related topics in the vocabulary section: Countries (5); numbers (11), personal details (5).

Where's the nearest police station?	Onde é a esquadra de polícia mais próxima?	*Onde eh a eshkwahdrah de poleesseeah maysh prosseemoo?*
Where is the nearest British[1] Embassy / Consulate?	Onde é a Embaixada Britânica / Consulado Britânico mais próximo?	*Onde eh ah embayshahdah breetahneekah / oo konsoolahdoo breetahneekoo maysh prosseemoo?*
I'd like to report a theft.	Quero participar um furto.	*Keroo pahrteesseepahr un~ foortoo.*
I was involved in an accident.	Estive envolvido num acidente.	*Eshteev'e envolveedoo noon~ asseedent'e.*
My ... has been stolen.	Roubaram-me o / a ...	*Rrohbahrawm~me oo/ah ...*

---

[1] To ask about other Embassies, see the list of countries in the Vocabulary section.

My car's been broken into.	Assaltaram-me o carro.	*Ahssahltahrawn~me oo kahroo.*
My child has walked off.	O meu filho desapareceu.	*Oo meyoo filyoo desahpahressayoo.*
His / her name is....	Chama-se ...	*Shahmah-sse ...*
He / She's .... years old, with blue / brown eyes and blond / brown / black, short / long, straight / curly hair	Tem ... anos, com olhos azuis / castanhos e cabelo loiro / moreno / preto /, curto / comprido.	*Teyn~ ahnoosh, kawn~ ohlyosh ahzooeesh / kahshtahnyoosh ee kabeloo loyroo / morenoo / pretoo /, coortoo / coompreedoo.*
Has a wallet / handbag / beach bag been handed in?	Foi entregue uma carteira / uma mala de mão /um saco de praia?	*Foy entregu'e ooma kahrtayrah / ooma mahlah de maw~ / oon~ ssahkoo de prayah?*

87

3 - VOCABULARY

1. Air travel

aircraft	avião	*ahvee**aw**~*
air hostess	hospedeira	*oshped**ay**rah*
airline	linha aérea	*l**ee**nyah ah**e**reah*
airport	aeroporto	*aherop**o**rtoo*
airport bus	autocarro do aeroporto	*aootok**a**hrroo doo aherop**o**rtoo*
arrival	chegada	*sheg**a**hdah*
baggage claim	recolha de bagagem	*rrek**o**lyah de bahg**a**hjayn~*
boarding card	cartão de embarque	*kahrt**aw**~ de embahrk'e*
captain	comandante	*komahnd**a**hnt'e*
ckeck-in	check-in	*shek-**ee**n*
crew	tripulação	*treepoolahss**aw**~*
customs	alfândega	*ahlf**a**hndegah*
delay	atraso	*ahtr**a**hzoo*

English	Portuguese	Pronunciation
departure	partida	*pahrteedah*
departure lounge	sala de embarque	*ssahlah de embahrk'e*
emergency exit	saída de emergência	*ssaheedah de emerjensseeah*
flight	voo	*vo-oo*
flight number	número de voo	*noomeroo de vo-oo*
gate	porta de embarque	*portah de embahrk'e*
jet	jacto	*jahktoo*
land	aterrar	*ahterrahr*
local time	hora local	*orah lokahl*
no smoking	não fumar	*naw~ foomahr*
non-smokers	não fumadores	*naw~ foomahdor'sh*
passenger	passageiro	*pahssahjayroo*
passport	passaporte	*pahssahport'e*
passport control	controlo de passaportes	*kontrol de pahssahport'sh*
pilot	piloto	*peelotoo*
runway	pista	*peeshtah*
seat	lugar	*loogahr*

3

89

seat belt	cinto de segurança	*sseentoo de ssegoorahnssah*
speed	velocidade	*velosseedahd'e*
steward	comissário de bordo	*komeessahreeoo de bordoo*
take off	descolar	*deshkolahr*
window	janela	*jahnelah*
wing	asa	*ahzah*

2. Cafés and restaurants

beer	cerveja	*sservejah*
bill	conta	*kontah*
bottle	garrafa	*gahrrahfah*
bowl	tigela	*teejelah*
cake	bolo	*bolo*
chef	cozinheiro	*kozeenhayroo*
coffee	café	*kahfeh*
cup	chávena	*shahvenah*
fork	garfo	*gahrfoo*
glass	copo	*kopoo*

knife	faca	*fahkah*
menu	ementa	*emehtah*
milk	leite	*layt'e*
plate	prato	*prahtoo*
receipt	recibo	*rresseeboo*
sandwich	sandes	*ssand'sh*
servicttc	guardanapo	*gwahrdahnahpoo*
snack	petisco	*peteeshkoo*
soup	sopa	*ssopah*
spoon	colher	*koolyer*
sugar	açúcar	*ahssookahr*
sweetencr	adoçante	*ahdossahnt'e*
table	mesa	*mezah*
tca	chá	*shah*
teaspoon	colher de chá	*koolyer de shah*
tip	gorjeta	*gorjetah*
waiter	empregado	*empregahdoo*
waitress	empregada	*empregahdah*

3

91

water	água	*ahgwah*
wine	vinho	*veenyoo*
wine list	lista de vinhos	*leeshtah de veenyoosh*

3. Camping

campsite	parque de campismo	*pahrk'e de kahmpeeshmoo*
backpack	mochila	*mosheelah*
blanket	cobertor	*kobertor*
caravan	caravana	*kahrahvahnah*
charges	tarifa	*tahreefah*
closed	fechado	*feshahdoo*
cooking utensils	utensílios de cozinha	*ootensseeleeoosh de kozeenyah*
drinking water	água potável	*ahgwah potahvel*
full	cheio	*shayoo*
ground sheet	lona impermeável	*lonah eempermeeahvel*
hitch-hike	pedir boleia	*pedeer bolayah*
how much?	quanto?	*qwahntoo?*

identity card	bilhete de identidade	*beelyet'e de eedenteedahd'e*
kitchen	cozinha	*kozeenyah*
light	luz	*loosh*
one night	uma noite	*oomah noyt'e*
one week	uma semana	*oomah ssemahnah*
public toilet	casa de banho pública	*kahzah de bahnyoo publeekah*
rope	corda	*kordah*
rubbish	lixo	*leeshoo*
saucepan	frigideira	*freejeedayrah*
shower	duche	*doosh'e*
sleeping bag	saco de cama	*ssahkoo de kahmah*
telephone	telefone	*telefon'e*
tent	tenda	*tendah*
tonight	hoje à noite	*oj'e ah noyt'e*
trailer	roulotte	*roolot'e*
youth hostel	pousada de juventude	*pohzahdah de jooventood'e*

3

4. Clothing

blouse	blusa	*bloozah*
bra	soutien	*ssooteeahn*
dress	saia	*ssahyah*
jacket	casaco	*kahzahkoo*
overcoat	sobretudo	*ssobretoodoo*
pants	cuecas	*kwekash*
shirt	camisa	*kaahmeezah*
shoes	sapatos	*ssahpahtoosh*
shorts	calções	*kahlssoyn~sh*
skirt	vestido	*veshteedoo*
slippers	chinelos	*sheeneloosh*
socks	peúgas	*pehoogahsh*
stockings	meias	*mayash*
suit	fato	*fahtoo*
swimsuit	fato de banho	*fahtoo de banyoo*
tie	gravata	*grahvahtah*

trousers	calças	*kahlssash*
underwear	roupa interior	*rrohpash*
vest	camisola interior	*kahmeezolah eentereeor*

5. Countries

Australia	Austrália	*Ahooshtrahleeah*
Austria	Áustria	*Áustreeah*
Belgium	Bélgica	*Beljeekah*
Canada	Canadá	*Kahnadah*
Denmark	Dinamarca	*Deenahmahrka*
England	Inglaterra	*Fenglahterrah*
Finland	Finlândia	*Feenlahndeeah*
France	França	*Franssah*
Germany	Alemanha	*Ahlemahnyah*
Greece	Grécia	*Gresseeah*
Holland	Holanda	*Olahndah*
Italy	Itália	*Italeeah*

3

Luxembourg	Luxemburgo	*Looshemboorgoo*
Ireland	Irlanda	*Eerlahndah*
New Zealand	Nova Zelândia	*Novah Zelahndeeah*
Norway	Noruega	*Norooehgah*
Scotland	Escócia	*Eskosseeah*
South Africa	África do Sul	*Ahfreekah de Ssool*
Spain	Espanha	*Eshpahnyah*
Sweden	Suécia	*Ssooesseeah*
The USA	Estados Unidos da América	*Eshtahdoosh Ooneedoosh dah Ahmehreekah*
Wales	País de Gales	*Paheesh de Gahl'sh*

6. Days, months, seasons and special dates

Sunday	Domingo	*Domeengoo*
Monday	Segunda-feira	*Segoondah-fayrah*
Tuesday	Terça-feira	*Terssah-fayrah*
Wednesday	Quarta-feira	*Qwahrtah-fayrah*

Thursday	Quinta-feira	*Keentah-fayrah*
Friday	Sexta-feira	*Seshtah-fayrah*
Saturday	Sábado	*Sahbahdoo*
January	Janeiro	*Jahnayroo*
February	Fevereiro	*Feverayroo*
March	Março	*Mahrssoo*
April	Abril	*Ahbreel*
May	Maio	*Mahyoo*
June	Junho	*Joonyoo*
July	Julho	*Joolyoo*
August	Agosto	*Ahgoshtoo*
September	Setembro	*Setembroo*
October	Outubro	*Ohtoobroo*
November	Novembro	*Novembroo*
December	Dezembro	*Dezembroo*
Spring	Primavera	*Preemahverah*
Summer	Verão	*Veraw~*
Autumn	Outono	*Ohtonoo*

3

English	Portuguese	Pronunciation
Winter	Inverno	*Invernoo*
Christmas Eve	Véspera de Natal	*Veshperah de Nahtahl*
Christmas Day*	Natal	*Nahtahl*
New Year's Eve	Véspera de Ano Novo	*Veshperah de Ahnoo Novoo*
New Year's Day*	Dia de Ano Novo	*Deeah de Ahnoo Novoo*
Carnival	Carnaval	*Kahrnahvahl*
Good Friday*	Sexta-feira Santa	*Seshtah-fayrah Ssahntah*
Easter Sunday	Domingo de Páscoa	*Domeengoo de Pahshkoah*
25th April*	Dia da Revolução	*Deeah dah Revoloossaw~ Veente sseenkoo de Ahbreel*
Labour Day*	1 de Maio	*Oon~ de Mahyoo*
Corpus Christi *	Corpo de Deus	*Korpoo de Deyoosh*
St. Anthony's Day (patron saint of Lisbon)	13 de Junho	*Trez'e de Joonyoo*

---

*National holidays

St. John's Day (patron saint of Oporto)	24 de Junho	*O veent'e sseenkoo de Joonyoo*
Camões Day*	10 de Junho	*Desh de Joonyoo*
Feast of the Assumption*	Dia da Assunção	*Deeah dah Ahssoonssaw~*
Restoration Day*	5 de Outubro	*Sseenkoo de Ohtoobroo*
All Saints' Day*	Dia de Todos-os-Santos	*Deeah de Todoos oosh Ssahntosh*
Republic Day*	1 de Dezembro	*Oon~ de Dezembroo*
Immaculate Conception*	8 de Dezembro	*Oytoo de Dezembroo*

3

Apart from these dates, 13th May has a special meaning for the Portuguese – it is the anniversary of the day when the Virgin appeared to three shepherd children in Fátima. During the previous weeks it is common to see pilgrims making their way towards the site along the main roads in central Portugal.

---

*National holidays

7. Food and drink

English	Portuguese	Pronunciation
almond	amêndoa	*ahmendoah*
apple	maçã	*massah~*
apricot	alperce	*ahlperss'e*
bean	feijão	*fayjoaw~*
beetroot	beterraba	*beterrahbah*
biscuit	biscoito	*beescoytoo*
black-eyed bean	feijão frade	*fayjoaw~ frahd'e*
breakfast	pequeno almoço	*pekenoo ahlmossoo*
cake	bolo	*boloo*
cheese	queijo	*kayjoo*
chick-pea	grão	*graw~*
chips	batata frita	*bahtahtah freetah*
cucumber	pepino	*pepeenoo*
chorizo sausage	chouriço	*shoreessoo*
coffee	café	*cahfeh*
dinner	jantar	*jahntar*

egg	ovo	*ovoo*
firewater	aguardente	*ahgwahrdent'e*
fish	peixe	*paysh'e*
garlic	alho	*ahyoo*
grape	uva	*oovah*
kidney bean	feijão encarnado	*fayjaw~*
lemon	limão	*leemaw~*
lettuce	alface	*ahlfass'e*
lunch	almoço	*ahlmossoo*
lupin	tremoço	*tremossoo*
meat	carne	*kahrn'e*
melon	melão	*melaw~*
milk	leite	*layt'e*
olive oil	azeite	*azayt'e*
omelette	omolete	*omolet'e*
onion	cebola	*ssebolah*
orange	laranja	*laharahnjah*

3

pea	ervilha	*erveelyah*
peach	pessego	*pessegoo*
pear	pêra	*perah*
pepper	pimenta	*peementah*
pineapple	ananás	*ananahsh*
potato	batata	*bahtahtah*
rice	arroz	*ahrrosh*
salt	sal	*ssahl*
sausage	salsicha	*ssahlsseeshah*
snail	caracol	*kahrahkol*
soft drink	refrigerante	*rrefreejerahnt'e*
sparkling water	água com gás	*ahgwah con~ gash*
still water	água sem gás	*ahgwah sayn~ gash*
sugar	açúcar	*assookahr*
supper	ceia	*ssayah*
tea	chá	*shah*
tomato	tomate	*tomaht'e*
vegetarian	vegetariano	*vejetahreeahnoo*

| water | água | *ahgwah* |
| watermelon | melancia | *melahnsseeah* |

8. Health

accident	acidente	*ahsseedent'e*
allergic	alérgico	*ahlerjeekoo*
ambulance	ambulância	*ahmboolahnsseeah*
anaemic	anémico	*ahnemeekoo*
anti-tetanus	anti-tétano	*ahntee-tetahnoo*
arm	braço	*brahssoo*
arthritis	artrite	*ahrtreet'e*
aspirin	aspirina	*ahshpeereenah*
asthma	asma	*ahshmah*
backache	dor nas costas	*dor nahsh koshtahsh*
bandage	ligadura	*leegahdoorah*
bite	picada	*peekahdoorah*
blister	bolha	*bolyah*

3

blood	sangue	*sahngu'e*
blood pressure	tensão arterial	*tenssaw~ ahrtereeahl*
blood test	análise ao sangue	*ahnaleese de sahngu'e*
bronchitis	bronquite	*bronkeet'e*
burn	queimadura	*kaymahdoorah*
chest	peito	*paytoo*
cold	frio	*freeoo*
(a) cold	uma constipação	*oomah konshteepahssaw~*
constipation	prisão de ventre	*preezaw~ de ventr'e*
contact lenses	lentes de contacto	*lent'sh de kontahktoo*
contagious	contagioso	*kontahjeeozoo*
corn	calo	*kahloo*
cough	tosse	*toss'e*
cut	cortar	*kortahr*
dentist	dentista	*denteeshtah*
diabetic	diabético	*deeahbeteekoo*
diarrhoea	diarreia	*deeahrrayah*
dizzy	com tonturas	*kom tontoorahsh*

doctor	médico	*medeekoo*
earache	dor de ouvidos	*dor de ohveedosh*
emergency services	serviços de urgência	*sserveessosh de oorjensseeah*
fever	febre	*febr'e*
filling	chumbo	*shoomboo*
finger	dedo	*dedoo*
first aid	primeiros socorros	*preemayros sokorros*
flu	gripe	*greep'e*
foot	pé	*pay*
fracture	fractura	*frahktoorah*
glasses	óculos	*okoolosh*
hay fever	febre do feno	*febr'e do fenoo*
headache	dor de cabeça	*dor de kahbessah*
health centre	centro de saúde	*ssentroo de ssahood'e*
heart	coração	*korahssaw~*
heart attack	enfarte	*enfahrt'e*
hospital	hospital	*oshpeetahl*

3

105

ill	doente	*dooent'e*
indigestion	azia	*ahzeeah*
injection	injecção	*eenjessaw~*
itch	comichão	*komeeshaw~*
kidney	rim	*rreen~*
leg	perna	*pernah*
lump	inchaço	*eenshahssoo*
migraine	enxaqueca	*enshahkekah*
nausea	náusea	*nahooseah*
neck	pescoço	*peshkossoo*
nurse	enfermeira	*enfermayrah*
operation	operação	*operahssaw~*
optician	oftalmologista	*oftahlmolojeeshtah*
pain	dor	*dor*
penicillin	penicilina	*peneesseeleena*
period pains	dores de período	*dor'sh de pereeodoo*
plaster	penso	*penssoo*

pneumonia	pneumonia	*pneyoomoneeah*
pregnant	grávida	*grahveedah*
prescription	receita médica	*ressaytah medeekah*
rheumatism	reumatismo	*reyoomahteeshmoo*
scald	escaldar	*eshkahldahr*
scratch	arranhão	*ahrrahnyaw~*
sore throat	dor de garganta	*dor de gahrgahntah*
splinter	estilhaço	*eshteelyahssoo*
sprain	entorse	*entorss'e*
sting	picada	*peekahdah*
stomach	estômago	*eshtomahgoo*
temperature	temperatura	*temperahtoorah*
toothache	dor de dentes	*dor de dent'sh*
travel sickness	enjoo	*enjo-oo*
ulcer	úlcera	*oolsseruh*
vaccination	vacina	*vahsseenah*
vomit	vomitar	*vomeetahr*

3

9. Hotels

balcony	varanda	*vahrandah*
bathroom	casa de banho	*kahzah de bahnyoo*
bed	cama	*kahmah*
bedroom	quarto de dormir	*qwahrto de dormeer*
bill	conta	*kontah*
breakfast	pequeno almoço	*pekenoo ahlmossoo*
cold water	água fria	*ahgwah freeah*
dining room	sala de jantar	*ssahlah de jahntahr*
dinner	jantar	*jahntahr*
double room	quarto de casal	*qwahrto de kahzahl*
early call	chamada para acordar	*shahmahdah pahrah ahkordahr*
foreign exchange	câmbio	*kahmbeeoo*
foyer	hall de entrada	*hawl de entrahdah*
full board	pensão completa	*pensaw~ kompletah*
ground floor	rés-do-chão	*rraysh do shaw~*

half board	meia pensão	*mayah pensaw~*
hot water	água quente	*ahgwah kent'e*
identity card	bilhete de identidade	*beelyet'e de eedenteedahd'e*
key	chave	*shahv'e*
lift	elevador	*elevahdor*
lounge	sala de estar	*ssahlah de eshtahr*
lunch	almoço	*ahlmossoo*
manager	gerente	*jerent'e*
one night	uma noite	*oomah noyt'e*
reception	recepção	*rressessaw~*
reserve	reservar	*rrezervahr*
restaurant	restaurante	*reshtahoorahnte*
room	quarto	*qwahrtoo*
room service	serviço de quartos	*sserveessoo de qwahrtosh*
satellite TV	TV por satélite	*teh-veh por ssahteleet'e*
shower	duche	*doosh'e*

3

single room	quarto individual	*qwahrtoo eendeeveedooahl*
switchboard operator	telefonista	*telefoneeshtah*
toilet	casa de banho	*kahzah de bahnyoo*
twin room	quarto com duas camas	*qwahrtoo kom dooahsh kahmahsh*

10. Motoring

boot	mala	*mahlah*
brake	travão	*trahvaw~*
breakdown	avaria	*ahvahreeah*
bus lane	via para transportes públicos	*veeah pahrah trahnsport'sh poobleekoosh*
car	carro	*kahrroo*
caravan	caravana	*kahrahvahnah*
coach	autocarro	*ahootokahrroo*
coach station	estação de autocarro	*eshtahssaw~ de ahootokahrroo*

corner	esquina	*eshkeenah*
crossroads	cruzamento	*kroozahmentoo*
dead end	sem saída	*ssen~ ssaheedah*
diesel	gasóleo	*gahzoleoo*
diversion	desvio	*deshveeoo*
drive	conduzir	*kondoozeer*
driver's licence	carta de condução	*kahrtah de kondoossaw*
end of motorway	fim da auto-estrada	*feen~ de ahooto-eshtrahdah*
engine	motor	*motor*
exhaust	tubo de escape	*tooboo de eshkahp'e*
fanbelt	correia da ventoinha	*korrayah dah ventoeenyah*
garage	estação de serviço	*eshtahssaw~ de sserveessoo*
gears	mudanças	*moodahnssahsh*
give way	dar prioridade	*dahr preeoreedahd'e*
headlights (dipped)	médios	*medeeosh*
headlights (full)	máximos	*mahsseemoosh*

3

111

heavy vehicle	veículo pesado	*vayeekooloo pezahdoo*
level crossing	passagem de nível	*pahssahjen~ de neevel*
lorry	camião	*kahmeeaw~*
mirror	espelho	*eshpelyoo*
motorbike	mota	*motah*
motorway	auto-estrada	*ahooto-eshtrahdah*
no parking	proibido estacionar	*proeebeedoo eshtahsseeonahr*
number plate	matrícula	*mahtreekoolah*
oil	óleo	*oleeoo*
on the left	à esquerda	*ah eshkerdah*
on the right	à direita	*ah deeraytah*
one-way	sentido único	*ssenteedoo ooneekoo*
pedestrian zone	zona pedonal	*zonah pedonahl*
petrol	gasolina	*gahzoleenah*
petrol station	estação de serviço	*eshtahssaw~ de sserveessoo*

puncture	furo	*fooroo*
queue	bicha, fila	*beeshah, feelah*
road	estrada	*eshtrahdah*
road closed	estrada vedada ao trânsito	*eshtrahdah vedahdah ao trahnzeetoo*
roadworks	obras na estrada	*obrahsh nah eshtrahdah*
sidelights	mínimos	*meeneemoosh*
skid	derrapar	*derrahpahr*
speed limit	limite de velocidade	*leemeet'e de velosseedahd'e*
steering wheel	volante	*volahnt'e*
straight on	em frente	*ayn~ frent'e*
toll	portagem	*portahjayn~*
tow	rebocar	*rrebokahr*
town centre	centro da cidade	*ssentroo duh sseedahd'e*
traffic jam	engarrafamento	*engahrrahfahmentoo*
traffic lights	semáforos	*ssemahforosh*

3

truck	camião	*kahmeeaw~*
tyre	pneu	*pneyoo*
tyre pressure	pressão de ar	*pressaw~ de ahr*
van	furgoneta	*foorgonetah*
wheel	roda	*rrodah*

11. Numbers - cardinals

1	um, uma	*oon~, oomah*
2	dois, duas	*doysh, dooahsh*
3	três	*tresh*
4	quatro	*qwahtroo*
5	cinco	*sseenkoo*
6	seis	*ssaysh*
7	sete	*sset'e*
8	oito	*oytoo*
9	nove	*nov'e*
10	dez	*desh*
11	onze	*onz'e*

12	doze	*doz'e*
13	treze	*trez'e*
14	catorze	*katorz'e*
15	quinze	*keen~z'e*
16	dezasseis	*dezahssaysh*
17	dezassete	*dezahsset'e*
18	dezoito	*dezoytoo*
19	dezanove	*dezahnov'e*
20	vinte	*veen~t'e*
21	vinte e um	*veen~t'e ee oon~*
22	vinte e dois	*veen~t'e ee doysh*
23	vinte c três	*veen~t'e ee tresh*
30	trinta	*treen~tah*
31	trinta c um	*treen~tah ee oon~*
40	quarenta	*qwarentah*
50	cinquenta	*sseenkwentah*
60	sessenta	*ssessentah*
70	setenta	*ssetentah*

3

80	oitenta	*oytentah*
90	noventa	*noventah*
100	cem	*ssayn~*
101	cento e um	*ssentoo ee oon~*
102	cento e dois	*ssentoo ee doysh*
200	duzentos	*doozentoosh*
300	trezentos	*trezentoosh*
400	quatrocentos	*qwatrossentoosh*
500	quinhentos	*keenyentoosh*
600	seiscentos	*sseishssentoosh*
700	setecentos	*ssetessentoosh*
800	oitocentos	*oytossentoosh*
900	novecentos	*novessentoosh*
1000	mil	*meel*
10000	dez mil	*dez meel*
20000	vinte mil	*veen~te meel*
21500	vinte e um mil	*veen~te e oon~ meel ee*
	e quinhentos	*keenyentoosh*

| 100000 | cem mil | *ssayn~ meel* |
| 1000000 | um milhão | *oon~ meelyaw~* |

- ordinals

1st	primeiro[1]	*preemayroo[1]*
2nd	segundo	*ssegoondoo*
3rd	terceiro	*terssayroo*
4th	quarto	*qwahrtoo*
5th	quinto	*keen~too*
6th	sexto	*ssextoo*
7th	sétimo	*sseteemoo*
8th	oitavo	*oytahvoo*
9th	nono	*nonoo*
10th	décimo	*desseemoo*
11th	décimo primeiro	*desseemoo preemayroo*
12th	décimo segundo	*desseemoo ssegoondoo*

3

[1] there are feminine forms to numbers (*primeira, segunda* etc., Monday, for instance is *segunda-feira*)

13th	décimo terceiro	*desseemoo terssayroo*
14th	décimo quarto	*desseemoo qwahrtoo*
15th	décimo quinto	*desseemoo keentoo*
16th	décimo sexto	*desseemoo ssaysstoo*
17th	décimo sétimo	*desseemoo sseteemoo*
18th	décimo oitavo	*desseemoo oytavoo*
19th	décimo nono	*desseemoo nonoo*
20th	vigéssimo	*veejezeemoo*
21st	vigéssimo primeiro	*veejezeemoo preemayroo*
22nd	vigéssimo segundo	*veejezeemoo segoondoo*
100th	centésimo	*ssentezeemoo*
1000th	milésimo	*meelezeemoo*

12. Personal details

| Family name[1] | Apelido | *ahpeleedoo* |
| First name | Nome | *nom'e* |

---

[1] The Portuguese often keep their mother's name and their father's – and maybe more. Their full name can therefore be up to seven or eight names.

118

Age	Idade	*eedahd'e*
Address	Morada	*morahdah*
Date of birth	Data de Nascimento	*dahtah de nahsheementoo*
Place of birth	Naturalidade	*natooraleedahd'e*
Nationality	Nacionalidade	*nasseeonahleedad'e*
Passport number	Número do passaporte	*noomeroo doo passaport'e*
Place and date of issue	Local e data de emissão	*locahl e datah de emeessaw~*

3

12. Public transport

booking office	bilheteira	*beelyetayrah*
buffet car	carruagem restaurante	*kahrrooahjayn~ reshtahoorahnt'e*
compartment	compartimento	*kompahrteementoo*
connection	ligação	*leegahssaw~*
departure	partida	*pahrteedah*
emergency switch	alarme	*ahlahrm'e*

entrance	entrada	*entrahdah*
exit	saída	*ssaheedah*
first class	primeira classe	*preemayrah klahss'e*
get in	entrar	*entrahr*
get out	sair	*ssaheer*
guard	guarda	*gwahrdah*
information	informações	*eenformahssoyn~sh*
left luggage	depósito de bagagens	*depozeetoo de bahgahjay~sh*
lost property	perdidos e achados	*perdeedoosh e ahshahdoosh*
luggage	bagagem	*bahgahjay~*
newspaper kiosk	quiosque	*keeoshk'e*
no smoking	proibido fumar	*proeebeedo foomahr*
platform	plataforma	*plahtahformah*
rail	carril	*kahrreel*
railway	caminho de ferro	*kahmeenyoo de ferroo*
return ticket	bilhete de ida e volta	*beelyet'e de eedah e voltah*

seat reservation	reservas	*rrezervahsh*
second class	segunda classe	*ssegoondah klahss'e*
single ticket	bilhete simples	*beelyet'e sseemplesh*
suitcase	mala	*mahlah*
ticket collector	revisor	*rreveezor*
timetable	horário	*horahreeoo*
track	via	*veeah*
traffic lights	semáforos	*ssemahforoosh*
train	comboio	*komboyoo*
tram	eléctrico	*elektreekoo*
waiting room	sala de espera	*ssahlah de eshperah*

3

14. Sending mail and communicating

addressee	destinatário	*deshteenahtahreeoo*
airmail	via aérea	*veeah ahereeah*
by e-mail	por e-mail	*por ee-mahyl*
collection	cobrança	*kobrahnssah*

121

counter	balcão	*bahlkaw~*
delivery	distribuição	*deeshtreebweessaw~*
fill in	preencher	*pree-ensher*
first-class mail	correio azul	*korrayo ahzool*
form	formulário	*formoolahreeoo*
letter	carta	*kahrtah*
letter box	marco do correio	*mahrkoo doo korrayoo*
money order	vale postal	*vahl'e poshtahl*
over the internet	pela internet	*pelah eenternet*
package	encomenda	*enkomendah*
post	correio	*korrayoo*
postage rates	tarifas postais	*tahreefahs poshtahysh*
postal order	vale postal	*vahl'e poshtahl*
postcard	postal	*poshtahl*
postcode	código postal	*kodeegoo poshtahl*
poste-restante	posta-restante	*poshtah-reshtahnt'e*
postman	carteiro	*kahrtayroo*
post office	correios	*korrayosh*

registered letter	carta registada	*kahrtah rejeeshtahdah*
recorded delivery	carta registada	*kahrtah rrejeeshtahdah*
	com aviso de recepção	*kom ahveezoo de rressessaw~*
short message service (SMS)	serviço de mensagens escritas (SME)	*sserveesso de menssah-jaynsh eshkreetahsh (SME)*
stamp	selo	*sseloo*
surface mail	via superfície	*veeah sooperfeessee'e*
telegram	telegrama	*telegrahmah*

15. Shopping

audio equipment	equipamento áudio	*ekeepahmentoo ahoodeeoo*
baker's	padaria	*pahdahreeah*
bargain	pechincha	*pesheenshah*
bookshop	livraria	*leevrahreeah*
boutique	boutique	*booteek'e*

123

butcher's	talho	*ta*hlyoo
buy	comprar	*kompra*hr
cake shop	pastelaria	*pahshtelahree*ah
cheap	barato	*bahra*htoo
chemist's	farmácia	*fahrmahsseeah*
department store	grande armazém	*grahnd'e ahrmahza**yn**~*
estate agent's	agência imobiliária	*ahjensseeah eemobee-leeahreeah*
fashion	moda	*mo*dah
fishmonger's	peixaria	*payshahree*ah
florist's	florista	*floree*shtah
go shopping	ir às compras	*eer ahsh kompra*hsh
grocer's	mercearia	*mersseahree*ah
household appliances	electro-domésticos	*elektro-domeshteekosh*
ironmonger's	loja de ferragens	*lo*jah de *ferrahja**yn**~sh*
ladies' wear	roupa de senhora	*rro*pah de ssenyo*rah*
men's wear	roupa de homens	*rro*pah dee *o*mayn~sh
newsagent's	tabacaria	*tahbahkahree*ah

out-of-town store	hipermercado	*eepermerkahdoo*
pre-payment	pré-pagamento	*preh-pahgahmentoo*
price	preço	*pressoo*
receipt	recibo	*rresseeboo*
record shop	loja de discos	*lojah de deeshkoosh*
sale	saldo	*ssahldoo*
shoe shop	sapataria	*sahpahtahreeah*
shop	loja	*lojah*
shopping centre	centro comercial	*ssentroo komersseeahl*
souvenir shop	loja de artesenato	*lojah de ahrtezenahtoo*
special offer	oferta limitada	*ofertah leemeetahdah*
spend	gastar	*gahshtahr*
stationer's	papelaria	*pahpelahreeah*
supermarket	supermercado	*ssoopermerkahdoo*
tailor	alfaiate	*ahlfahyaht'e*
till	caixa	*kahyshah*
till receipt	recibo de caixa	*resseeboo de kahyshah*
toy shop	loja de brinquedos	*lojah de breenkedoosh*

125

| travel agent | agência de viagens | *ahjensseeah de veeahjayn~sh* |

16. Sports

athletics	atletismo	*ahtleteeshmoo*
ball	bola	*bolah*
beach	praia	*prahyah*
bicycle	bicicleta	*beesseekletah*
boat hire	aluguer de barcos	*ahloogu'er de bahrkoosh*
danger	perigo	*pereegoo*
dive	mergulhar	*mergoolyahr*
diving board	prancha de saltos	*prahnshah de sahltosh*
fishing	pesca	*peshkah*
fishing rod	cana de pesca	*kahnah de peshkah*
flippers	barbatanas	*bahrbahtahnahsh*
football	futebol	*footebol*
football match	jogo de futebol	*jogoo de footebol*
golf	golfe	*golf'e*

golf course	campo de golfe	*kahmpoo de golf'e*
gymnastics	ginástica	*jeenahshteekah*
hockey	hóquei	*okay*
jogging	jogging	*jogueen~*
lake	lago	*lahgoo*
lifeguard	nadador-salvador	*nahdahdor-ssahlvahdor*
mountaineering	alpinismo	*ahlpeeneeshmoo*
no camping	proibido acampar	*proeebeedoo ahkahmpahr*
no swimming	proibido nadar	*proeebeedoo nahdahr*
oxygen bottle	garrafa de oxigénio	*gahrrahfah de okseege-neeoo*
pedal boat	gaivota	*gahyvotah*
race	corrida	*korreedah*
racket	raqueta	*rrahketah*
riding	equitação	*ekeetahssaw~*
rowing boat	barco a remos	*bahrkoo ah rremoosh*
run	correr	*korrer*
sailboard	prancha de windsurf	*prahnshah de weendsoorf*

127

sailing	velejar	*fahzer velah*
sand	areia	*ahrayah*
sea	mar	*mahr*
skate	patinar	*pahteenahr*
skates	patins	*pahteensh*
snorkel	respirador aquático	*reshpeerahdor ahqwahtee-koo*
stadium	estádio	*eshtahdeeoo*
suntan lotion	bronzeador	*bronzeeahdor*
swim	nadar	*nahdahr*
swimming pool	piscina	*peessheenah*
tennis	ténis	*teneesh*
tennis court	campo de ténis	*kahmpoo de teneesh*
tennis racket	raqueta de ténis	*rrahketah de teneesh*
tent	tenda	*tendah*
tide (high, low)	maré (alta, baixa)	*mahreh (ahltah, bahyshah)*
underwater fishing	pesca submarina	*peshkah soobmahreenah*
volleyball	voleibol	*volaybol*

water-skiing	esqui aquático	*eshkee ahqwahteekoo*
wave	onda	*ondah*
wet suit	fato isotérmico	*fahtoo eesotermeekoo*
windsurfing	windsurf	*weendsoorf*
yacht	iate	*eeaht'e*

3

17. Telephoning

call	chamada	*shahmahdah*
code	código	*kodeegoo*
dial	marcar	*mahrkahr*
dialling tone	sinal	*sseenahl*
emergency	urgência	*oorjensseeah*
enquiries	informações	*eenformahssoyn~sh*
extension	extensão	*eshtensaw~*
international call	chamada internacional	*shahmahdah*
		eenternahsseeonahl
number	número	*noomeroo*
operator	telefonista	*telefoneeshtah*

129

pay phone	telefone público	*telefon'e poobleekoo*
receiver	auscultador	*ahooshkooltahdor*
reverse charge call	chamada paga	*shahmahdah pahgah*
	no destinatário	*noo deshteenahtahreeoo*
telephone directory	lista telefónica	*leeshtah telefoneekah*

18. Telling the time

one o'clock	uma hora	*oomah orah*
five past one	uma e cinco	*oomah ee sseenkoo*
a quarter past two	duas e um quarto	*doysh ee oon~ qwahrtoo*
half past three	três e trinta	*tresh ee treentah*
twenty to four	vinte para as quatro	*veent'e pahrah ahsh qwahtroo*
a quarter to five	um quarto para as cinco	*oon~ qwahrtoo pahrah ahsh sseenkoo*
2 pm / 14:00h	catorze horas	*kahtorzee orahsh*

130

half past three in the afternoon / 15.30	quinze e trinta	*keenz'e ee treentah*
a quarter to seven in the evening / 18.45	dezoito e quarenta e cinco / um quarto para as sete	*dezoytoo ee qwahrentah eesseenkoo / oon~ qwahrtoo pahrah ahsh set'e*
mid-day / noon	meio-dia	*mayoo deeah*
midnight	meia-noite	*mayah noyt'e*

3

19. Time prases

at the moment	neste momento	*nesht'e momentoo*
day	dia	*deeah*
early	cedo	*ssedoo*
fortnight	quinzena	*keenzenah*
half an hour	meia hora	*mayah orah*
hour	hora	*orah*
in 1989	em mil novecentos e oitenta e nove	*ayn~ meel novessentoosh ee oytentah ee nov'e*

in three days	dentro de três dias	*dentroo de tresh deeahsh*
last night	ontem à noite	*ontayn~ ah noyt'e*
last week	a semana passada	*ah ssemahnah pahssahdah*
last year	o ano passado	*oo ahnoo pahssahdoo*
late	tarde	*tahrd'e*
minute	minuto	*meenootoo*
month	mês	*mesh*
next week	a semana que vem	*ah ssemakenah ke vayn~*
next year	o ano que vem	*oo ahnoo ke vayn~*
quarter of an hour	um quarto de hora	*oom kwahrtoo de orah*
second	segundo	*segoondoo*
this afternoon	esta tarde	*eshtah tahrd'e*
this evening	esta noite	*eshtah noyt'e*
this morning	esta manhã	*eshtah mahnya~*
this week	esta semana	*eshtah semahnah*
today	hoje	*oj'e*
tomorrow	amanhã	*ahmahnya~*
tomorrow morning	amanhã de manhã	*ahmahnya~ de mahnya~*

tonight	hoje a noite	*oj'e ah noyte*
two days ago	há dois dias	*ah doysh deeahsh*
year	ano	*ahnoo*
yesterday	ontem	*ontayn~*

20. The Weather

3

bad weather	mau tempo	*mahoo tempoo*
breeze	brisa	*breezah*
cold weather	tempo frio	*tempoo freeoo*
cloud	nuvem	*noovayn~*
dry weather	tempo seco	*tempoo ssekoo*
earthquake	tremor de terra	*tremor de terrah*
fair or fine weather	bom tempo	*bon~ tempoo*
fog	nevoeiro	*nevooayroo*
hail	granizo	*grahneezoo*
hurricane	furacão	*foorahkaw~*
ice	gelo	*jeloo*

lightning	raio, faísca	*rahyoo, faheeshkah*
warm weather	tempo quente	*tempoo kent'e*
wet weather	tempo húmido	*tempoo hoomeedoo*
wind	vento	*ventoo*
mist	neblina	*nebleenah*
rain	chuva	*shoovah*
rainbow	arco-íris	*ahrkoo eereesh*
rainy weather	tempo chuvoso	*tempoo shoovozoo*
snow	neve	*nev'e*
storm	temporal	*temporahl*
tempest	tempestade	*tempeshtahd'e*
thunder	trovão	*trovaw~*

4 - SOME TYPICAL PORTUGUESE DISHES

In the section below you will find soups, starters, main courses and desserts. The selection will help you choose what you would like from looking at a menu in a restaurant window. Apart from complete meals, there are various things worth trying, such as light snacks in bars – the ubiquitous *prego no pão* (a piece of steak in a bread roll), *uma bifana* (slices of pork in a bread roll), *salgadas* (savouries) and *sandes mista* (ham and cheese in a roll). A large coffee and milk is *um galão* and *um carioca de chã* is a hot infusion made from pouring boiling water over slices of lemon rind. *Bom apetite!*

4

Soups

Caldo verde – Green soup

Finely chopped green kale (known in Portugal as Portuguese cabbage) cooked in a thick broth of mashed potatoes and onions, seasoned with olive oil and usually served with a slice of chorizo sausage in it.

Canja de galinha – Chicken broth

A tasty soup containing rice or pasta, pieces of shredded chicken, and maybe an onion boiled in the stock from cooking the bird.

Puré de legumes – Vegetable purée soup

In-season vegetables – potatoes, carrots, cabbage, onion etc. – boiled and puréed along with a dash of olive oil.

Sopa à alentejana – Soup Alentejo style

Garlic, coriander and salt to taste are blended or mashed in a mortar, scalded with boiling water and the mixture poured over a slice of bread in an individual bowl. A lightly poached egg is added while the liquid is still very hot.

Sopa da pedra – Soup with a stone[1]

A thick soup cooked with red beans, onion, diced potatoes, bacon and sausages, seasoned with olive oil, pepper and coriander, garnished with pieces of shredded meat.

---

[1] The name is said to derive from a wandering monk who took a clean round stone with him and when he was given board, he asked his hosts if they knew how to make soup from a stone. He washed the stone, boiled some water, added the stone and asked if they had some vegetables or meat he could add – potatoes, beans, onions, pieces of ham etc.

Sopa de tomate

Tomato pieces and slices of onion and potato cooked in a stock of olive oil, bay leaves and spicy herbs. Served with thick slices of day-old farmhouse bread, with a poached egg, traditionally cooked in the soup itself.

Starters and main dishes

Açorda de marisco – Shellfish in savoury bread pudding

A soft bread pudding prepared with the broth from boiling the shellfish and seasoned with olive oil, garlic, chilli and coriander. Prawns, clams and mussels are folded into the mixture and while it is still piping hot, one egg per person is added and stirred in briskly.

Alheira de Mirandela – Garlic sausage Mirandela style[1]

A soft sausage made from poultry, rabbit and soaked bread, seasoned with pepper, paprika and garlic (alho – hence the name). Served with a fried egg and chips.

---

[1] Tradition has it that this is a sausage invented during the Inquisition by Jewish "converts", who could claim that it was made with pork, like other sausages. Therefore, they could eat it and show they were not Jews.

Ameijoas à Bulhão Pato – Clams Bulhão Pato style

Fresh clams served in a sauce of olive oil and chopped garlic, seasoned with pepper, coriander and lemon juice and served as a starter.

Arroz de tamboril – Angler fish with rice

Pieces of fish stewed with rice in a sauce of olive oil, onion, garlic, bay leaf, parsley, fish stock and pepper. Sprinkled with chopped parsley and topped with prawns.

Bacalhau – Cod

When the Portuguese talk of cod, they invariably mean dried cod, soaked in water for at least 24 hours with a minimum of two changes of water, and the last soak may be in milk, depending on the recipe. There are said to be 101 ways of preparing cod, and if you want to be adventurous, try asking for *bacalhau à casa* (the cook's own special style). Among the many options to be found in restaurants, two of the more popular dishes are described here.

Bacalhau à Brás – Dried cod Bras style

Made with flaked cod, slender strips of potatoes and sliced onions, cooked in olive oil, garlic and pepper. Whisked eggs are folded in as binding. Sprinkled with chopped parsley and garnished with black olives.

Bacalhau à Zé do Pipo – Dried cod Zé do Pipo style

Cod cut into pieces, boiled in milk, placed in an earthenware bowl with a layer of onion gently fried in olive oil and seasoned with pepper and bay leaf. The mixture is covered with mashed potatoes and cooked in the oven until golden brown, topped off with mayonnaise and garnished with black olives.

Cabrito à padeiro – Roast kid baker's style

Pieces of kid seasoned with crushed garlic, bay leaf, pepper, paprika, white wine and roasted in the oven together with potatoes, thin slices of onion and slices of bacon.

4

Caldeirada à pescador – Fisherman's hot pot

Eels, mullet, skate and a choice of other white fish cooked in layers in an earthenware casserole with onions, sliced potatoes, tomatoes, garlic, bay leaf, olive oil and parsley. Served with slices of toasted bread.

Carne de porco à alentejana

Chunks of lean pork fried with diced potatoes and cockles or clams in a sauce of lard, garlic, red pepper pulp, bay leaf and pepper, sprinkled with coriander. Served with chopped Portuguese-style pickles and slices of lemon.

Cozido à portuguesa

A mixture of boiled beef, slices of chicken, pig's trotters, smoked ham, black pudding, chorizo sausage and *farinheira* (a sausage made of pork fat, flour and spices), cooked in a pan along with a variety of vegetables that usually includes carrots, potatoes, cabbage and turnip. Accompanied by rice cooked separately.

Dobrada à moda do Porto – Tripe Oporto style

A stew consisting of veal tripe, calf's foot, pig's head, chicken, white haricot beans and carrots, cooked with olive oil, lard, onion, garlic, bay leaf and black pepper, sprinkled with cummin and chopped parsley. Accompanied by dry white rice.

Feijoada à transmontana – Bean stew Trás-os-Montes style

A mixture of beans, pig's ear, pig's trotters, smoked ham and sausage, occasionally with white cabbage, cooked in olive oil and seasoned with garlic, chilli pepper and bay leaf. Served with rice.

Frango no churrasco – Grilled chicken

Chick opened lengthwise, flattened and grilled over the coals, basted with a sauce of olive oil, chopped garlic and hot pepper. Served with chips and salad.

Lampreia à moda do Minho – Lamprey Minho style

Slices of lamprey marinaded with red wine, the blood of the fish, pepper, garlic, parsley and bay leaf. Olive oil is added to the liquid and the fish is cooked in it. Served with rice and toasted bread.

Lagosta suada à moda de Peniche – Lobster Peniche style

Lobster cut across the rings and slowly stewed in a sauce from the rest of the lobster, margarine, olive oil, tomato, garlic, white wine, a dash of brandy and port wine, chilli, pepper and nutmeg. Served garnished with the feelers, claws and pincers of the lobster.

4

Leitão à moda da Bairrada – Roast suckling pig Bairrada style

The suckling pig is rubbed with a paste of crushed garlic, fat bacon, red pepper, bay leaf and white wine and roasted on a spit over charcoal. Served with thin-sliced fried potatoes and a separate salad.

Sardinhas assadas – Grilled sardines

The fish is sprinkled with rock salt and grilled over charcoal. Taken straight to table where it is served with boiled potatoes and a salad made of tomatoes and lettuce. Grilled red or green peppers to accompany. If the fish is really fresh, the skin should peel off easily.

Truta à transmontana – Trout Trás-os-Montes style

Fried trout with a filling of chopped smoked ham, served with a sauce of melted butter, lemon juice and chopped garlic.

Desserts

Arroz doce – Rice pudding

Rice cooked in milk, sugar, egg yolk and rind of lemon. Served cold, sprinkled with powdered cinnamon.

Bolo de bolacha - Biscuit cake

A creamy paste made of crumbled biscuits, cream, sugar and vanilla and drops of lemon juice. Served in slices.

Bolo de mel – Walnut and honey cake

Traditional cake from Madeira made with wheat flour, sugar, butter, lard, walnuts, almonds, molasses and oranges. Spiced with Madeira wine, aniseed and cinnamon.

Leite creme – Creamy custard

A creamy mixture of milk, sugar, custard, egg yolk and lemon rind, powdered with sugar and browned with a red-hot iron.

Pastel de Nata – Custard tart

Puff pastry with a filling of custard cream browned in the oven in small tins, served with ground cinnamon to be sprinkled over the top to taste.

4

Tigeladas – Sweet bowls

Milk, egg and flour pudding cooked in the oven in individual earthenware bowls.

Toucinho do céu – Heavenly-sweet bacon

A cake made of egg yolk, almonds, butter, sugar, wheat flour and pumpkin jam. Spiced with cinnamon and clove and sprinkled with castor sugar.

5 - CONVERSION TABLES

Distances

Kms	1	2	3	4	5	6	7	8	9	10
Kms → Miles	0.62	1.24	1.86	2.48	3.11	3.73	4.35	4.97	5.59	6.21
Miles	1	2	3	4	5	6	7	8	9	10
Miles → Kms	1.61	3.22	4,83	6.44	8.05	9.66	11.27	12.88	14.49	16.10

Weights

kg	1	2	3	4	5	6	7	8	9	10
kg → lbs	2.20	4.41	6.61	8.82	11.02	13.23	15.43	17.63	19.84	22.04
lbs	1	2	3	4	5	6	7	8	9	10
lbs → kg	0.45	0.91	1.36	1.81	2.27	2.72	3.17	3.62	4.08	4.53

Temperatures

°C	-10	0	5	10	20	30	36.9	40	100
°F	14	32	41	50	68	86	98.4	104	212

Liquids

gals.	1	2	5	10	20	30	50
gals. → ltrs	0.22	0.44	1.10	2.20	4.40	6.60	11.00
gals. → ltrs	1	2	5	10	20	30	50
ltrs → gals.	4.54	9.10	22.73	45.46	90.92	136.4	227.3

Tyre pressures

lb → in^2	18	20	22	24	26	28	30	33
kg → cm^2	1.3	1.4	1.5	1.7	1.8	2.0	2.1	2.3

Women's dresses and suits

UK	10	12	14	16	18	20
Europe	36	38	40	42	44	46
USA	8	10	12	14	16	18

5

Men's suits and clothes

UK/USA	36	38	40	42	44	46
Europe	46	48	50	52	54	56

Shoes

UK	4	5	6	7	8	9	10	11
Europe	37	38	39	41	42	43	44	45
USA	5 1/2	6 1/2	7 1/2	8 1/2	9 1/2	11	13	15

Men's shirts

UK/USA	14	14 1/2	15	15 1/2	16	16 1/2	17
Europe	36	37	38	39	41	42	43

Women's sweaters

UK/USA	32	34	36	38	40
Europe	36	38	40	42	44

Waist and chest measurements

Inches	28	30	32	34	36	38	40	42	44	46
Cms	71	76	80	87	91	97	102	107	112	117

6 - USEFUL TELEPHONE NUMBERS[1]

Airport (Lisbon) - arrivals and departures 218 413 700
Citizens' Advice Bureau - 808 241 107
Coastguard Service (Lisbon) - 214 401 919
International Calls through the Operator[2] - 171
International Code 00 (for the Country and Area Codes, consult the
Telephone Directory)
International Telegrams[2] - 1582
National Information Service - 118
Police Service (Lisbon) - 218 641 000
Reverse Charge call[2] - 120
Tourist Information Office - (Lisbon) 213 463 314
Tourist Information Service[2] - 800 296 296
Weather situation and forecast[2] - 12 400
Yellow Pages over the phone - 707 202 222

6

---

[1] These numbers are correct at the time of printing.
[2] Call is free

7 - LEARNING AND IMPROVING

The idea behind this part of the book is to give you the opportunity to broaden and deepen your knowledge of the language. There are four sections:

A - A very simplified grammar, which will help you go beyond merely repeating phrases from the book.

B - Some of the most useful words for a visitor, to serve as a basis which you can learn and then use to develop your knowledge of the language.

C - A list of fundamental language functions to enable you to situate yourself quickly in everyday situations.

D - Some tips on picking up the language. Most of these are obvious, but their value cannot be over-stressed.

A. Grammar

1. Nouns, articles and adjectives

1.1. <u>Nouns</u> are either masculine (ending in -*o*) or feminine (ending in -*a*)[1]. (See Reference Chart 1a.) The plural is formed by simply adding-s. (Chart 1b.) [2]

1.2. <u>Articles</u> (**a/the/some**) are placed before the noun, as are the <u>adjectives</u> for **this/that/these/those.** (Rows 1 and 2)

1.3. <u>Numbers</u> will also be found in the Columns **2** and **6**. Note that there are two forms of the number **2** (*dois / duas*).

1.4. Other <u>adjectives</u> are normally placed after the noun. They change according to number and gender and therefore an adjective like *fresco*, **chilled**, has four forms: *fresco, fresca, frescos, frescas*. (Rows 4 and 8) Adjectives ending -e (such as *quente*, **hot**) have only two forms, singular and plural (Row 4 and 8).

---

[1] There are a few exceptions (the most useful to remember are *o dia, o problema* and *o clima*).

[2] The most common exceptions are nouns ending -*ão*, for which there are different plurals, best learnt individually: *alemão* (German) - *alemães*; *mão* (hand) - *mãos*; *condição* (condition) -*condições*.

Reference chart 1a
(Singular nouns and adjectives, Columns 2, 3 and 4)

Column / Row	1 Verb	2 a / one / the / this / that	3 noun (sing.)	4 adjective
1	*Quero*	*um / o / este / aquele*	*bolo.*	
2	*Quero*	*uma / a / esta / aquela*	*bebida.*	
3	*Quero*	*um*	*sumo*	*fresco.*
4	*Quero*	*uma*	*bebida*	*fresca.*
5	*Quero*	*um* *uma*	*bolo* *bebida*	*quente.*

Reference chart 1b
(Plural nouns and adjectives, Columns 6, 7 and 8)

Colum \ Row	5 Verb	6 some / the / these / those /number	7 noun (plu.)	8 adjective
1	*Quero*	*uns / os / estes / aqueles / dois*	*bolos.*	
2	*Quero*	*umas / as / estas / aquelas / duas*	*bebidas.*	
3	*Quero*	*dois*	*sumos*	*frescos.*
4	*Quero*	*duas*	*bebidas*	*frescas.*
5	*Quero*	*dois* *duas*	*bolos* *bebidas*	*quentes.*

2. Pronouns

As can be seen in Chart 1 (Columns 1 and 5), there is no absolute need for a *subject pronoun* (**I / you / he, she, it / we / they**). The verb ending is usually enough to indicate the subject. *Quero* and *Eu quero* are both correct, but the second is more emphatic. Check Point 6 (page156) to get the verb endings right.

Reference chart 2

	Person	Subject	Object[1]	Strong form[2]
Singular	1st (I, me)	*eu*	*me*	*mim*
	2nd (you - friendly)	*tu*	*te*	*ti*
	2nd you - formal)	*você*[3]	*o, a*	*ele, ela*
	3rd (he, she, it; him, her, it)	*ele, ela*	*o,a*	*ele, ela*
Plural	1st (we, us)	*nós*	*nos*	*nós*
	2nd (you)	*vocês*[3]	*vos*	*vocês / vos*
	3rd (they, them)	*eles, elas*	*os, as*	*eles, elas*

[1] A more detailed grammar must be consulted for specific forms and uses of object pronouns.
[2] Used for example with prepositions – see Point 3 below.
[3] See "Levels of formality" (Point 9) for more detail.

3. **Prepositions**

These are important to express such ideas as **with him, for us, by airmail, to Lisbon**

The most important are: *a* (to) *antes de* (before), *com* (with), *de* (of, from), *depois de* (after), *em* (in), *para* (for), *por* (by), *sem* (without), *sobre* (on).

*Vou **com** ele.* – I am going with him.

*Há uma mensagem **para** nós?* – Is there a message for us?

*Quero enviar uma carta **por** via aérea.* – I want to send a letter by airmail.

*Vamos **a** Lisboa amanhã.* – We are going to Lisbon tomorrow.

4. **Some common combinations involving prepositions**

Reference chart 3

In the	*no*	*na*	*nos*	*nas*
On the	*no*	*na*	*nos*	*nas*
In this /these	*neste*	*nesta*	*nestes*	*nestas*
In that / those	*naquele*	*naquela*	*naqueles*	*naquelas*
Of the	*do*	*da*	*dos*	*das*
By the	*pelo*	*pela*	*pelos*	*pelas*
In some	*nalgum*	*nalguma*	*nalguns*	*nalgumas*
To the	*ao*	*à*	*aos*	*às*
With me /us	*comigo*		*connosco*	

5. Verbs - groups

Portuguese verbs can be divided into three groups depending on the ending of the base or infinitive form: *-ar (falar), -er (comer), -ir (partir)*.

Below there is a table of the three groups, showing the main tenses in the <u>first person singular</u>.

Reference chart 4

	First group		Second group		Third group	
Infinitive	*falar*	to speak	*comer*	to eat	*partir*	to leave
Present	*falo*	I speak	*como*	I eat	*parto*	I leave
Past Continuous[1]	*falava*	I was speaking	*comia*	I was eating	*partia*	I was leaving
Past	*falei*	I spoke	*comi*	I ate	*parti*	I left
Future	*falarei*	I'll speak	*comerei*	I'll eat	*partirei*	I'll leave
Conditional	*falaria*	I would speak	*comeria*	I would eat	*partiria*	I would leave
Past Participle	*falado*	spoken	*comido*	eaten	*partido*	left
Gerund	*falando*	speaking	*comendo*	eating	*partindo*	leaving

[1] Known in Portuguese as *o passado imperfeito* (the imperfect).

6. Verbs - endings and tenses

The most important endings are the first and third person (remember that the polite form of address uses the third person (*Que quer comer?* – **What do you want to eat**?)

In the chart below, the first and third persons are given, with the <u>past</u>, <u>present</u> and the <u>future</u>.[1] The most common <u>future form</u> uses *ir* + main verb.

Reference chart 5

Present	*falo / fala /* *falamos / falam*	*como / come /* *comemos / comem*	*parto / parte /* *partimos / partem*
Past	*falei / falou /* *falámos / falaram*	*comi / comeu /* *comemos / comeram*	*parti / partiu /* *partimos / partiram*
Future (with *ir*)	*vou / vai / vamos* *vão falar*	*vou / vai / vamos /* *vão comer*	*vou / vai / vamos* *vão partir*

[1] The future form *falarei, falará, falaremos, falarão* is rarely used. If you are interested in its forms and uses, you should consult a detailed grammar.

156

7. **Specific verbs: *ser, estar, ter, ir* and *haver; poder* and *dever.*** [1]

1. *Ser* and *estar* both mean **to be**, *ser* for permanent situations (I am English: ***sou inglês***) and ***estar*** for temporary situations (I am tired: ***estou cansado***)

2. *Ter* is used for compound tenses (*tenho visto* - I have seen) [2]

3. *Vou* (from *ir*) is a common alternative to the future (*vou fazer* - I am going to do)

4. *Haver* is mainly found in the equivalent of **there is, there are**: *há.* There is only one form, for singular and plural.

5. *poder* (**can, may**, indicating possibility or ability or permission)

6. *dever* (**must, should**, indicating duty or giving advice)

---

[1] The first five can be either <u>main verbs</u> or <u>auxiliary verbs</u>. The other two are <u>modal verbs</u>. A more detailed grammar must be consulted for the different uses in the two languages.

[2] If you are interested in these tenses, you should consult a detailed grammar.

8. Negatives

The negative is formed by putting *não* before the verb, as in *Não vou* (I don't go, I'm not going).

9. Levels of formality

The Portuguese can be very formal, especially in the early stages of getting to know you. They may use the *tu* form (normally reserved for close friends and family) or *você* (you, more formal), or even a third person form, such as *o senhor* or your name.

In a shop, you will probably hear:

Que é que o senhor / a senhora procura / deseja / pretende? – What are you looking for? / What would you like?

If you are known by name, you will be addressed in the third person, with o/a before your name:

Onde é que a Jessica quer ir? – Where would you like to go, Jessica?
Onde é que o Jason quer ir? – Where would you like to go, Jason?

Section B – Some useful words

6.1 - Adjectives

beautiful - bonito	empty - vazio	old - velho
big - grande	first - primeiro	red - vermelho
black - preto	free - livre	short - curto
blue - azul	green - verde	small - pequeno
busy - ocupado	hot - quente	strong - forte
cheap - barato	last - último	ugly - feio
cold - frio	long - comprido	weak - fraco
dear (or loved)-querido	new - novo	white - branco
expensive - caro	next - próximo	young - jovem, novo

6.2 - Nouns and pronouns

beach - praia	car - carro	coffee - café
beer - cerveja	card - cartão	day - dia
book - livro	child - criança	dinner - jantar

drink - bebida
doctor - médico
everybody - toda a gente
fine - multa
food - comida
handbag - mala
health - saúde
luggage - bagagem
lunch - almoço
money - dinheiro
magazine - revista
map - mapa

newspaper - jornal
night - noite
nobody - ninguém
nothing - nada
passport - passaporte
return - volta
room - quarto
shop - loja
somebody - alguém
something - algo, alguma coisa
somewhere - nalgum lado

stamp - selo
suitcase - mala de viagem
tea - chá
ticket - bilhete
time - tempo, hora
town - vila / cidade
train - comboio
water - água
weather - tempo
wine - vinho

6.3 - Question words

How? - Como?
How much? - Quanto?
How old? - Quantos anos?

What - Que?
When? - Quando?
Where? - Onde?

Where ... from? - Donde?
Who? - Quem?
Why? - Porquê?

6.4 - Verbs (apart from those in Section A)

to catch - apanhar	to hear - ouvir	to speak - falar
to come - vir	to know - conhecer, saber	to stay - ficar
to do - fazer	to leave - partir	to study - estudar
to drive - conduzir	to live - viver, morar	to take - tomar
to find - achar, encontrar	to meet - encontrar	to think - pensar
to finish - acabar, terminar	to pull - puxar	to understand - perceber,
to get - apanhar (= catch);	to push - empurrar	entender
receber (= receive)	to put - pôr	to walk - ir a pé
to get to - chegar a	to read - ler	to write - escrever
to go - ir	to see - ver	

Section C – Some basic language functions

Apologising	Peço (imensa) desculpa
Asking for agreement	Concorda? Acha boa ideia?
Asking for help	Desculpe, pode ajudar-me?

Asking someone about their job	E o senhor / a senhora, que é que faz / onde é que trabalha?
Asking what someone thinks about an idea	Que é que acha?
Asking what something costs	Quanto é? Quanto custa?
Asking what something is called	Como é que se chama isto?
Attracting someone's attention	Por favor / Com licença
Giving information about yourself	Sou / Estou
Making a suggestion	Podemos ir / fazer...
Saying goodbye	Adeus / Tchau / Até logo
Saying hello (depending on the time of day)	Bom dia / Boa tarde / Boa noite
Saying thank you	Obrigado / Obrigada
Talking about your job or studies	Trabalho / Estudo em / na / numa

Section D - Some tips on picking up the language

- Do a short language course if possible before you go on a visit (or before you go again!).

- Get to know some people as soon as you settle (e.g. go to the same café regularly if you're staying in one place for any length of time, get to know people on the camp-site or on the beach).

- Use the basics as quickly as possible (saying "thank you", pointing to something in a café and asking what it's called etc).

- Take a small dictionary with you.

- Read a newspaper every day; ask your friends to explain things.

- Watch television, especially the news.

- Films on TV and at the cinema are normally sub-titled so listen and try to connect wh you hear with what you see at the bottom of the screen.

- After you learn something, introduce it into a conversation as quickly as you can.